REVELATION
READY

PREPARING FOR NOW

REBEKAH ARIAS

FIRST EDITION

ISBN: 978-1-946466-21-1

Library of Congress Control Number: 2017955529

Published by

Certa
PUBLISHING

P.O. Box 2839, Apopka, FL 32704

Printed in the United States of America

Acknowledgments

I am grateful to my heavenly Father, for entrusting me with this task and giving me the strength to see it through. Thank you for being there for me, particularly during the still, long night hours. Thank you for your faithfulness and for helping me do what I could never have done on my own. May this book bring honor and glory to Your name.

Secondly, thank you to my darling husband, Alejandro, for believing in me and believing in this project. Your own perseverance and the belief that with God, anything is possible, continually inspires me. Thank you for listening to the hours of musings and deliberations over the past four years, and for encouraging me to keep writing when I felt like giving up! I love you with all my heart!

To my sweet girl Carielle: I have fond memories of writing the first few chapters of *Revelation Ready* in the moments I could manage to tear my eyes off your sleeping newborn face! Thank you for being such a patient girl through this process. You bring Daddy and me so much joy; you are the "fizz" in our lives! Lots of hugs and kisses.

A huge thanks to Jaana Puronpaa, Elizabeth Noble, and Julie Harriman, who tirelessly gave of their time and energy to invest in this book, and to our friends at Certa Publishing.

Lastly, thank you to my wonderful family and friends, to everyone who has supported and encouraged me in this endeavor; I am truly grateful.

Contents

PART FOUR: Becoming Revelation Ready

❖ ❖ ❖

Introduction

"You want me to what, Lord?"

"Write a book on Revelation," He impressed on me again.

I had been half-asleep, but now I was wide-awake. A thousand thoughts raced through my mind—what a challenging topic to write on, how I could possibly fit a book into my schedule, and how utterly unqualified I felt for the task. The list went on and on.

God has been faithful to me, however, and the book you are holding in your hands is evidence of His grace and strength. It is my sincere desire that this book would be a blessing to you, as you face the challenging times we are living in. Before you "dive in" though, here are a couple of things I would like to share with you.

Preparation and Purpose in the Last Days

This book has two primary purposes. The first is to equip and prepare believers for the times we are living in. Every time you turn on the television and watch the news, you would doubtless notice the turmoil and shaking happening in the world. Every day, a piece of the "Revelation puzzle" is put in place. The whole picture is being completed at an astonishing speed. Now, more than ever, we must be equipped with a clear sense of spiritual direction and the knowledge of our place in this chapter of world history.

The second reason this book was written is to stir you into action, to fulfill your God-given calling. *Revelation Ready* is a wake-up call, a challenge to walk in holiness and purpose. It is the call to take hold of every opportunity to snatch souls from the jaws of hell, while we still have time.

Post-trib, mid-trib…?

There are a whole host of end-time theologies for believers to choose from—pre-tribulational, post-tribulational, mid-tribulational, post-millennial, millennial, futurist, etc. etc. The list is endless. There are those who believe in the rapture, those who believe only in the second coming of Christ, and those who believe in elements of both. For the purposes of this book, I will not be subscribing explicitly to any of these views. It is my desire that the broader message of this book would be unfettered by complex doctrine and dogma.

Part Two of *Revelation Ready* is devoted to the signs of the last days. Again, although some of my personal convictions regarding these signs will inevitably become obvious as you read, I urge you not to lose sight of the book's overall message if your own beliefs differ. My analysis of the signs is meant to present a range of theories concerning how they might be fulfilled, not dogmas.

A Springboard

Lastly, I pray that you would be inspired to grapple with the concepts we cover and to conduct your own investigation into them. In this way, guided by the Holy Spirit, you can begin to unearth God's truths for yourself. Hopefully, this book will act as a springboard—a starting point for receiving the personal revelations God wants to give to you.

PART ONE:

A Message in the Night

❖ ❖ ❖

Chapter 1

The Dream

I did not recognize the woman as anyone I knew, nor did I know
her name. In spite of this, we laughed and talked like old friends,
and instinctively I felt that she was a dear friend, a sister in Christ. We
were on the upper floor of a house, getting ready for some kind of event.
Although I did not know what the occasion was, there was an air of
expectation, the sense that it was very special. In a wardrobe nearby,
hung two magnificent ball gowns, the most dazzling I had ever seen. In
the midst of our preparations, my friend suddenly turned and rushed to
an open window, shouting excitedly, "He's here; He's coming!"

My excitement evaporated, turning into panic. I was not ready
and had yet to change into my gown. Rushing to the wardrobe, I quickly
pulled it on and ran to the window to join my friend. Looking out, I
saw a huge cloud formation in the sky—the billowing, meringue-like
variety you might see forming over the mountains of a tropical country.
A dazzling light, as bright as the sun, seemed to emanate from within
the cloud. As my eyes adjusted, I saw the face and likeness of Jesus in
the light. His face shone, not just with the light's radiance, but with
pure majesty. As the cloud descended towards the earth, Jesus seemed
to notice my friend and I standing in the window. I was surprised and
delighted when He smiled and waved to us. Surprised, because even in
His glorified form He still radiated such love for people. I felt the same

as one might feel, seeing a loved one again for the first time in decades. An indescribable elation flooded my heart, bubbling over into laughter. Especially touching to me, was the way that Jesus looked genuinely overjoyed to see us.

Like a movie, the scene cut to a completely new one. I suddenly found myself in a large auditorium. It was shaped like a hall, long and rectangular. It went back as far as the eye could see and was brimming with people. The hall was divided into two sections. At the front of the building, a small group of people sat quietly, their attention directed toward the front. My friend and I sat in this section. Behind us, I noticed an aisle separating us from the rows behind, like you might see in a cinema.

In direct contrast to our group, those seated behind us were noisy and active. Parents scolded their children, who bickered loudly over a box of popcorn. Friends sat chatting and laughing, and a few of the women were absorbed in their handbags, sifting through the contents as though searching for misplaced items. A few latecomers continued to drift in. Everyone seemed to be completely preoccupied with their own affairs.

I directed my attention back to the front and noticed, for the first time, Jesus standing before all the people. His aspect was very different from the last time I had seen Him—He was silent and still as He surveyed the crowd. His expression was calm and solemn, powerful. His eyes reminded me of the intense gaze of a reposing lion, observing its surroundings. A peace emanated from Jesus—there was the sense that He could be stern if He wanted to, but that He had utter dominion over all things. He was flanked by dozens of angels and a handful of men that I sensed were Biblical figures. Like noble members of a royal court, they stood silently alongside Jesus, watching the crowd.

Then something very odd dawned on me. I realized that the people seated in the section behind us did not seem to see or even notice Jesus. It was as though He was invisible to them. My friend and I became so alarmed by this, that we could not stay silent. "We are servants of the

Most High!" we yelled over the noise, "and He is Jesus!" My friend pointed to the front, "He is the Son of the Living God, and He has come back, just as He said He would!" While the vast majority of people ignored us or didn't seem to hear, eventually a handful began to take notice, looking up with dazed expressions. They looked as though they had awoken from a deep sleep, or had stepped from a dark room into broad daylight.

After a moment, one man's look of bewilderment turned to a sneer. "That's not Jesus!" He yelled scornfully. "That's a hologram! This whole thing is a joke. Come on kids, let's go!" With that, he grabbed his children's hands and dragged them out of their seats, toward the exit. As I watched, I felt a deep sense of alarm. Somehow I knew that if they walked out, they would never have the opportunity to re-enter the auditorium. There was a finality about leaving.

To my horror, other people began to make similar remarks and move towards the exits.

"When does the show start? This is ridiculous!"

"We're leaving right now."

"I can't wait around all day!"

What started as a trickle became droves, as people flowed steadily toward the exits. Frantic by this stage, my friend and I shouted, "Stop! No! Please—don't go, you don't know what you are doing! Please!" We stood on our chairs and faced the crowd, pleading with them until we had shouted ourselves hoarse. Few paid any attention.

Finally, I broke down in tears as the horrible realization dawned on me—"I saw them!" I said to my friend, "every day, on the streets, in the shops, in the public places, I saw them—but I didn't warn them!" My shoulders shook, gripped by uncontrollable sobs. "It's too late now—it's too late!" I felt a grief greater than anything I had ever felt in my life. The feeling grew stronger until it was literally too much.

Overwhelmed, I either fainted or fell into a deep sleep. As I fell backward off my chair, I felt a soft, strong pair of arms reach out and catch me. For a split second, my viewpoint shifted to the third person—

allowing me to see the angel who had caught me, as he gently placed me on the ground. Laying there with my eyes closed, I continued to murmur, "It's too late, too late…"

I awoke with a gasp, my lips still forming the words and my heart pounding. Despite having been asleep for hours, I was instantly wide-awake.

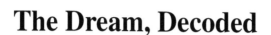

Chapter 2

The Dream, Decoded

Before exploring the dream's meaning, I feel the need to clarify what it is *not*. It is not meant to be taken in any way as doctrine or a literal representation of the coming of Christ, the rapture, or the day of judgment. My sense is that many of the elements in the dream are prophetic, symbolic and metaphorical in nature. I do not see the second part of the dream, for example, as a literal picture of the day of the Lord. Rather than trying to decipher the specific events the dream might depict, I believe it is more important to focus on the messages communicated through its symbolism.

Getting Ready

At the beginning of the dream, I saw my friend and I getting ready. This speaks of preparation on two levels. Firstly, it represents the bride of Christ (the church), getting ready to meet Him, as described in Revelation:

> Let us rejoice and be glad and give him glory! For the wedding of the Lamb has come, and his bride has made herself ready. *(Revelation 19:7)*

Just as my friend and I put on our finest gowns, Jesus longs for

His spotless bride, to be ready for Him. She is to be without spot and blemish, radiant and holy. Secondly, this aspect of the dream speaks of the need for Christians to prepare for Jesus' return on a personal level. We need to be dedicated to living a life of intimacy with God, our hearts fully prepared to meet Him at any moment. It has been Jesus' desire since the foundation of the world for us to stand before Him and see Him face to face. It is that desire, the very same that drove Him to the cross, that I saw expressed in His face.

A Shocking Revelation

I thought I knew what the "scene," in the auditorium represented—it seemed straightforward enough. When God gave me extra insight, however, the revelation He gave me shook me to the core. I had assumed that I knew the identity of the people seated in the hall. It was obvious to me—those seated quietly with their eyes fixed on Jesus were believers, while those who were seated behind us were not. The scene was a metaphor for the "sheep" being separated from the "goats," spoken of by Jesus:

> When the Son of Man comes in his glory, and all the angels with him, he will sit on his glorious throne. All the nations will be gathered before him, and he will separate the people one from another as a shepherd separates the sheep from the goats. He will put the sheep on his right and the goats on his left. (Matthew 25:31–33)

I was wrong. When God revealed to me the true identity of those seated in the back part of the hall, I was stunned. "Those in the second group are not all unbelievers." I felt the Spirit say to me. "What! What do you mean, Lord?" I asked. "Not all of those seated in the second group are unbelievers—in fact, some of them are 'believers'." I felt the grief in His words.

As I meditated on this new information, the dream began to take on a whole new meaning. Alarmingly, I now understood that many of those who seemed to be in their own world were in fact distracted believers. Blinded by their preoccupations and wrapped up in the busyness of their own affairs, they had completely missed Jesus standing right in front of them.

The activities the crowd concerned themselves with took on specific meanings, symbolic of areas that can keep us from pursuing God wholeheartedly. Hunting through purses and wallets represented being consumed by money and material gain, chatting to others represented being engrossed in social lives and relationships, and bickering with children and spouses represented obsessing over family life and ignoring the things of God.

Those who sat quietly, on the other hand, their gazes fixed on Jesus, represented those who are truly devoted to Him. Putting away all distractions, they were attentive to any slight movement Jesus made, like a stoic army, waiting for their commander's orders. An atmosphere of worship emanated from this group—their deep love for Him was palpable.

I recalled the bizarre comment made by one man, declaring that Jesus was no more than a hologram. Interestingly, the suffix "–gram" comes from the Greek word *gramma*, meaning; "something written, a message." To this man, the message (the gospel) was no more than a "hollow-gram"—a powerless version of the Word. He had never *known* the Word in the first place. It was then that I understood that those who got up and walked out of the auditorium are the people who will walk away from the faith. Without being strongly rooted in a true relationship with Jesus Christ, they will choose instead to pursue the things of the world.

As they left the hall, I had cried out to them, urging them to stay. The profound sadness I felt and the regret of not reaching out to them when I had the chance, has come to impact me deeply today. Dear Friend, those who left the hall were not ready to see Jesus. *"Are you ready?"*

PART TWO:

Know the Signs

❖ ❖ ❖

Chapter 3

The Temple Reborn

Traveling and ministering internationally is a tremendous blessing, and I feel privileged to be able to have a "bird's eye view," of what God is doing among His people across the globe. It is wonderful to be able to meet our international brothers and sisters and get to know the "family members" we never knew we had. I love to sit late into the night, talking about the things of God with them and hearing what He is laying on their hearts. These conversations often give a fascinating insight into what God is saying to His people corporately.

We have noticed that there are prophetic "seasons," for example, when God chooses to communicate a specific message to His children. Many of the people we meet do not, of course, know or have any contact with each other. This makes it all the more astonishing when we hear a believer from Colombia say the same thing as a believer from Poland, or a believer from Wisconsin say the same as a believer from Nigeria. God's prophetic word transcends geography, resonating through His whole body to those who are listening.

To our amazement, we have seen a distinct shift over the past few years in what many are sensing in their spirits. There is a building sense of urgency, and we regularly find ourselves hearing statements like:

"We are living in the last days."

"We do not have much time left."

"Things are changing very quickly."

Like a seismograph, such remarks point to the spiritual and physical tremors beginning to shake the nations, the events that we now find ourselves in the thick of. The signs of the last days are all around us, we only need to open our eyes.

Lamentably, there are many who (understandably) are wary of end-time predictions and prophecies. Perhaps this can be attributed, in part, to a string of wrong predictions, particularly since the year 2000—the Y2K millennium bug scare, the 2011 end of the world prediction by Harold Camping and the Mayan apocalypse in 2012—to name a few. There is a danger that such "false alarms" desensitize us to true prophecy. The danger then becomes another extreme—to dismiss all predictions as "conspiracy theory." We must remember that the Enemy's forte has always been to create counterfeits of the real thing—and what better way than to disorientate the children of God than with false predictions? In this way, the Enemy seeks to throw believers "off the scent," keeping them in the dark about the true spiritual hour. The Enemy knows that his time is short. If anything, we can be encouraged by the increase in false predictions—especially as they are a key indicator that we are living in the last days; "...many false prophets will appear and deceive many people" (Matthew 24:11).

As false prophecies and predictions abound, we must not fall into the trap of becoming apathetic. With the Bible firmly in our hands and our hearts attuned to the Spirit's voice, we must carefully weigh the signs of the times. Even then, we must avoid the other extreme—of putting more emphasis on the signs, than the One who created the signs. Signs should ultimately lead us to a closer, holier, deeper walk with God. We must understand that He has created these signs to protect His people and warn the world, through us.

Signs of the Last Days

Bible prophecy is being fulfilled before our eyes at such a rate, that I literally can't keep up with the significant signs unfolding on a daily basis. For this reason, the following section will only ever be a snapshot, not a comprehensive list of end-time signs.

Rebuilding the Temple

> Concerning the coming of our Lord Jesus Christ and our being gathered to him, we ask you, brothers and sisters, not to become easily unsettled or alarmed by the teaching allegedly from us—whether by a prophecy or by word of mouth or by letter—asserting that the day of the Lord has already come. Don't let anyone deceive you in any way, for that day will not come until the rebellion occurs and the man of lawlessness is revealed, the man doomed to destruction. He will oppose and will exalt himself over everything that is called God or is worshiped, so that he sets himself up in God's temple, proclaiming himself to be God. (2 Thessalonians 2:1–4)

This passage speaks of one of the key signs of the end of the age—the rebuilding of the temple in Israel. These words were first written by Paul to the church in Thessalonica, addressing a rumor that had been circulating among the believers, that the day of the Lord had already come. He reassured them that it had not come and that this sign was yet to be fulfilled. One of these signs will be the coming of the Man of Lawlessness (the Antichrist) who will set himself up in the temple, claiming to be God. Only then will the end come. For the Man of Lawlessness to fulfill this prophecy, we can infer that there must be a temple standing in the last days.

Daniel also foretold the rebuilding of the temple:

> The end will come like a flood: War will continue until the end, and desolations have been decreed. He will confirm a covenant with many for one 'seven.' In the middle of the

'seven' he will put an end to sacrifice and offering. And at the temple he will set up an abomination that causes desolation, until the end that is decreed is poured out on him.
(Daniel 9:26–27)

Some suggest that Daniel's prophecy has already been fulfilled, through one of two events: The desecration of the temple by Antiochus IV Epiphanes in 168BC, or its destruction by the Romans in 70AD. While these events seem to fit, neither meets the necessary criteria. To qualify as "the abomination that causes desolation," the event must:

a) Put an <u>end</u> to sacrifice in the temple, *and,*

b) <u>Set up</u> an abomination in the temple.

The Hebrew word used for abomination in Daniel 9:27 is *shiqquts,* meaning "a detestable idol."[1] Antiochus IV Epiphanes set up an idol in the temple (an image of the Greek god Zeus), but he did not succeed in putting an end to temple sacrifice—at least not permanently. In 164, during the Maccabean revolt, Antiochus' pagan altar was torn down, the temple was reconsecrated, and sacrifice resumed. During His earthly ministry, Jesus referred to Daniel's prophecy as an *event yet to come*;

So when you see standing in the holy place "the abomination that causes desolation," spoken of through the prophet Daniel—let the reader understand—then let those who are in Judea flee to the mountains. (Matthew 24:15–16)

Although the temple's destruction in 70AD effectively put an end to sacrifices, it did not result in an idol being set up. It had been the intention of the Roman general Titus to do so, but his plans were thwarted when the temple was set on fire, against his wishes. Although a temple to Jupiter was eventually built on the site, housing a statue of the god, this did not fulfill Scripture in the sense that the idol was set up *in* the holy sanctuary—the Jewish temple was no longer standing. It is also worth noting that neither Antiochus nor Titus made the prescribed seven-year peace covenant (Daniel 9:27).

A third theory exists, that the Dome of the Rock *is* the abomination of desolation. The problem is, this theory also fails to fulfill the necessary criteria. When the Dome of the Rock was built in 691AD, the temple had not been rebuilt since its destruction in 70AD, and sacrifices remained halted. Logically, the building of the Dome of the Rock could not stop sacrifices that were not being offered.

The Temple Today

As well as interpreting the Word directly, it is also important to be mindful of any current events that may point to Bible prophecy. There are, for example, some fascinating developments taking place in Israel concerning the temple. The fervent desire of many Jews to see the temple be rebuilt led to the establishment of *The Temple Institute*.[2] Since 1987, the Institute has been working towards re-instating temple service, a goal that seems closer today than ever before.

The Temple Institute has crafted authentic instruments for use in the Third Temple, made to the exact specifications given in the Bible. The priestly garments, the menorah, the incense altar and the table of showbread are some of the items that have already been replicated. Donors have the option to give the Mosaic half-shekel temple contribution or to contribute silver or gold to be melted down and used in the Temple.

Many Christians have become passionate to see the temple rebuilt.

A number of prominent ministers have upheld the cause, promoting it as one that *all* Christians should support—particularly those concerned about Israel's welfare. Potential supporters are sometimes told (directly or indirectly) that their contribution will somehow speed Christ's return. In our zeal to see our Lord, however, I believe it is of utmost importance that we thoroughly investigate the temple sign and understand what it means.

The Messiah — to be Revealed or Returning?

When Jesus returns, He will not need an earthly temple (although the temple's rebuilding will precede His coming.) The Word tells us that Jesus' throne is a heavenly, not an earthly one;

> The Son is the radiance of God's glory and the exact representation of his being, sustaining all things by his powerful word. After he had provided purification for sins, he sat down at the right hand of the Majesty in heaven. So he became as much superior to the angels as the name he has inherited is superior to theirs. For to which of the angels did God ever say, "You are my Son; today I have become your Father"? But about the Son he says, "Your throne, O God, will last for ever and ever; a scepter of justice will be the scepter of your kingdom. To which of the angels did God ever say, "Sit at my right hand until I make your enemies a footstool for your feet"? (Hebrews 1:3–5,8,13)

After Jesus overcame sin and death on the cross, He sat down at the right hand of the Father in heaven. He will be seated there (not on earth) until the Enemy is totally destroyed and the Antichrist is overthrown.

> For He must reign until He has put all His enemies under His feet. The last enemy to be destroyed is death. (1 Corinthians 15:25–26)

> And then the lawless one will be revealed, whom the Lord Jesus will overthrow with the breath of his mouth and destroy by the splendor of his coming. (2 Thessalonians 2:8)

It is, in fact, the Antichrist who will be using the Third Temple, making it his headquarters. It could be that he will one day allow the Jewish people to return to the temple and openly practice Mosiac law—a move that would undoubtedly gain him great favor and lead to widespread deception.

It is possible that when the Antichrist comes, he will seem to fulfill all prophetic prerequisites to be Israel's redeemer. Driven by his desire to enthrone himself on God's holy mountain and exalt himself, he will appear to esteem the temple. He will be seen as tolerant and will bring peace—for a time. Ultimately though, this peace will be shattered, as the "Man of Lawlessness" reveals his true colors.

> And through his policy also he shall cause craft to prosper in his hand; and he shall magnify himself in his heart, and by peace shall destroy many: he shall also stand up against the Prince of princes; but he shall be broken without hand. (Daniel 8:25, KJV)

Temple Sacrifice

The rebuilding of the temple is inextricably tied to reinstating temple sacrifice—something that ought to be a problematic consideration for Christians. It begs the question—why would we want to resurrect a practice that was abolished by the *ultimate* sacrifice—Jesus' death on the cross? Under the old covenant, ritual sacrifice and the law served to highlight the need for redemption and the futility of trying to atone for our own sins:

> The law is only a shadow of the good things that are coming—not the realities themselves. For this reason it can never, by the same sacrifices repeated endlessly year after year, make perfect those who draw near to worship. Otherwise, would they not have stopped being offered? For the worshipers would have been cleansed once for all, and would no longer have felt guilty for their sins. But those sacrifices are an annual reminder of sins. It is impossible

for the blood of bulls and goats to take away sins. (Hebrews 10:1–4)

First he said, "Sacrifices and offerings, burnt offerings and sin offerings you did not desire, nor were you pleased with them"—though they were offered in accordance with the law. Then he said, "Here I am, I have come to do your will." He sets aside the first to establish the second. And by that will, we have been made holy through the sacrifice of the body of Jesus Christ once for all. (Hebrews 10:8–10)

Under the new covenant, we have no need of sacrifice, having been justified by Jesus' blood.

Wanted: Temple Building Site

The greatest obstacle facing supporters of the Third Temple is the issue of *where* it would be built. The possible future location has been strongly contested, especially as the Dome of the Rock's position on the Temple Mount poses a significant challenge—that is, if the Dome of the Rock is actually situated on the site of the Second Temple. Some suggest that it is *not* and that the original temple's location actually lies elsewhere. One proposed site is based on the location of a cistern, believed to be used by priests for daily purification rituals.

The location identified by Professor Joseph Patrich of the Hebrew University Institute of Archaeology places the Temple and its corresponding courtyards, chambers, and gates in a more southeasterly and diagonal frame of reference than have earlier scholars.

In spotting the Temple in this way, Patrich concludes that the rock, over which the Dome of the Rock mosque was built in the 7th century C.E. is outside the confines of the Temple.[3]

If Patrich is correct, then it may be "easier" for the temple to be rebuilt than previously thought—it would no longer be tied up with the Dome of the Rock's location. Only time will tell exactly *how* the temple will be rebuilt, but one thing is for certain—very serious commitments are being made to this end. These things in mind, the likelihood of the temple being rebuilt in our lifetime is closer each day.

Israel's Ultimate Destiny

Lastly, it must be emphasized that, although many Jews rejected Jesus as Messiah, they are still part of God's end-time plan. There has been a subtle deception that has crept into the church—that Israel has somehow been replaced by the church as God's chosen people. Although "replacement theology" is seldom preached outright, it is present largely through omission—through the failure to acknowledge and embrace Israel's prophetic destiny. The danger of such an omission is that it flirts with that very same question Satan asked Eve in the garden of Eden; "Did God really say?" There is no way we can attempt to sweep aside the many binding promises made by God to Israel—the Word does not permit it. God has declared His faithfulness to Israel over and over, like an unending love letter.

"Though the mountains be shaken and the hills be removed, yet my unfailing love for you will not be shaken nor my covenant of peace be removed," says the Lord, who has compassion on you. (Isaiah 54:10)

"Only if these decrees vanish from my sight," declares the Lord, "will Israel ever cease being a nation before me." This is what the Lord says: "Only if the heavens above can be measured and the foundations of the earth below be searched out will I reject all the descendants of Israel because of all they have done," declares the Lord. (Jeremiah 31:36–37)

Clearly, God's covenant with His chosen nation is still binding. In spite of the events to come, there is yet a glorious season God has appointed for His people, one of restoration and salvation. God will not allow Israel to be consumed in the last days. I believe that one of the last, most powerful revivals is about to come to pass and that many Jews will at last enter the new covenant, through Yeshua:

> Again I ask: Did they stumble so as to fall beyond recovery? Not at all! Rather, because of their transgression, salvation has come to the Gentiles to make Israel envious. But if their transgression means riches for the world, and their loss means riches for the Gentiles, how much greater riches will their full inclusion bring! (Romans 11:11–12)

———— ❖ ❖ ❖ ————

Chapter 4

Unholy Alliances

What is ecumenism? A Christian buzzword? An ideal all believers should strive for? Or something else? It is important we know, especially as the ecumenical movement gains momentum and widespread favor in the church. Perhaps this is because of the positive connotations it carries—after all, isn't it the call to unity in the body of Christ? What's more, there are many Scriptures that seem to advocate ecumenism:

> Make every effort to live in peace with everyone and to be holy; without holiness no one will see the Lord. See to it that no one falls short of the grace of God and that no bitter root grows up to cause trouble and defile many. (Hebrews 12:14–15)

> My prayer is not for them alone. I pray also for those who will believe in me through their message, that all of them may be one, Father, just as you are in me and I am in you. May they also be in us so that the world may believe that you have sent me. I have given them the glory that you gave me, that they may be one as we are one—I in them and you in me—so that they may be brought to complete unity.

Then the world will know that you sent me and have loved them even as you have loved me. (John 17:20–23)

To find out if the Bible does, in fact, exhort us to ecumenism, we need to firstly study the word's origins. Derived from the Latin word *oecumenicus*, ecumenical actually means "universal." The original Greek word, *oikoumenikos*, means; "from or open to the whole world." Therefore, to be ecumenical is to unite under one banner, as a universal, worldwide church.

Unity through the Spirit

While a single, cohesive church without denominational barriers may sound like a noble aim, it is nonetheless fraught with danger. The principle danger of ecumenism is that it is a man-made concept, rather than a biblical one. Ecumenism is often the construct of man's organization and maneuvering, as opposed to the unity that only the Holy Spirit brings:

Make every effort to keep the unity of the Spirit through the bond of peace. There is one body and one Spirit, just as you were called to one hope when you were called (Ephesians 4:3–4)

Have you ever seen the triangle illustration sometimes used in marriage seminars? It shows a husband and wife at the two widest points of a triangle and God at the top. As the couple seeks God and draws nearer to Him, they ultimately grow closer to each other. This concept can also apply to the body of Christ. If we seek God, we will naturally become more united with one another. As the Holy Spirit fills and sanctifies us, traits such as malice, selfishness, and resentment are stripped from our hearts. Walls come down, as God fills us with His love. Just as there is no division between Jesus, the Father and the Holy Spirit, so God's children will become one.

Ecumenism, on the other hand, often operates with compromise—under the guise of "tolerance." As the church dilutes biblical truth and surrenders godly convictions, it risks becoming "unequally yoked." In direct contrast to biblical unity, this often leads believers one step closer to the world, rather than towards God. When the Holy Spirit is not behind the push for unity, those who are not in the same spirit are joined in unholy alliances.

Do not Judge?

One of the loudest cries in our politically correct society has become, "don't judge!" The media, in particular, has propagated the belief that to think differently to another person or group is to pass judgment on them. When a Christian is seen to be "judging," many would respond: "Didn't Jesus say not to judge?" (on the basis of Matthew 7:1, *"Do not judge, or you too will be judged."*) While this verse seems self-explanatory, as is the case with all verses, it is important to look at the Scripture in its entirety. Right after Jesus said, *"Do not judge,"* He spoke specifically about the *kind* of judgment He was referring to. He urged people to take the plank out of their eye before removing the plank from their neighbors (see Matthew 7:2–5). The point was to avoid judgment based on religious hypocrisy.

There is, however, another kind of judgment—one that Jesus encourages us to use. *Righteous* judgment is to discern between right and wrong. Jesus said, *"Why don't you judge for yourselves what is right?"* (Luke 12:57). He exhorted us to make moral distinctions. We are to discern between sound and unsound doctrine, what is holy and unholy. If we separate ourselves from those who practice false doctrine and embrace sin, it is not out of condemnation, but to make a stand for righteousness. In this way, we also guard our hearts and minds.

I urge you, brothers and sisters, to watch out for those
who cause divisions and put obstacles in your way that are

contrary to the teaching you have learned. Keep away from them. (Romans 16:17)

He [the overseer] must hold firmly to the trustworthy message as it has been taught, so that he can encourage others by sound doctrine and refute those who oppose it. (Titus 1:9, emphasis added)

Today the word judgment has become a euphemism for "condemnation." If a believer perceives sin, they are seen to be condemning. There is a difference, however, between right judgment and condemnation. *Critical judgment* passes judgment in the spirit of condemnation and self-righteousness, while *righteous judgment* loves all that is holy and just and is done in humility and love.

The Next Step

From ecumenism to the interfaith movement is not a flying leap, it is a natural progression. Once the foundation of the Word is compromised by shifting convictions, it becomes easy to "unite" Christianity with world religions. The product of this unholy alliance is embodied in a figure so horrifying, that even the apostle John was dumbfounded:

One of the seven angels who had the seven bowls came and said to me, "Come, I will show you the punishment of the great prostitute, who sits by many waters. With her the kings of the earth committed adultery, and the inhabitants of the earth were intoxicated with the wine of her adulteries." Then the angel carried me away in the Spirit into a wilderness. There I saw a woman sitting on a scarlet beast that was covered with blasphemous names and had seven heads and ten horns. The woman was dressed in purple and scarlet, and was glittering with gold, precious stones and pearls. She held a golden cup in her hand, filled with abominable things and the filth of her adulteries I saw that the woman was drunk with the blood of God's holy people, the blood of those who bore testimony to Jesus. When I saw her, I was greatly astonished. (Revelation 17:1–4, 6)

To discover the woman's identity, we need to scour the Bible for other instances of the same symbol (an effective strategy for unlocking prophetic motifs). Throughout the Word, we see symbolic representations of women. The nation of Israel is often referred to as a wife, for example:

> For your Maker is your husband—the Lord Almighty is his name—the Holy One of Israel is your Redeemer; he is called the God of all the earth. The Lord will call you back as if you were a wife deserted and distressed in spirit—a wife who married young, only to be rejected," says your God. (Isaiah 54:5–6)

A woman can also represent the church:

> Husbands, love your wives, just as Christ loved the church and gave himself up for her to make her holy, cleansing her by the washing with water through the word, and to present her to himself as a radiant church, without stain or wrinkle or any other blemish, but holy and blameless. (Ephesians 5:25–27)

Conversely, a harlot (such as Gomer, the prophet Hosea's wayward wife) represents those who have strayed from their covenant relationship with God, Though an actual person, Gomer became a living metaphor of Israel's unfaithfulness towards God. The prostitute/unfaithful people metaphor is also used in Ezekiel chapter 16. From these passages, we can infer that the Harlot of Revelation represents:

a) those who have turned their back on God, and,

b) a counterfeit of those who belong to God.

The Harlot of Revelation is none other than the apostate church. She is a twisted anti-church, a perversion of the pure and spotless bride of Christ (see Revelation 19:7). Chapter 17 unlocks much of the symbolism surrounding her. The many waters she sits upon represent: *"peoples, multitudes, nations, and languages"* (*v.* 15). She is a false religious system with global influence, who colludes with those in power (*v.* 2) and relentlessly persecutes the true church (*v.* 6). Those who take part in her adulteries appear *"intoxicated"* (*v.* 2). Not only is she powerful, but she is rich —well dressed, glittering with gold, precious stones and pearls (*v.* 4). Her immense wealth comes from her alliance with the Beast, who has outfitted her with all she needs to fulfill her evil plans. She also represents the *"great city,"* that will be her global headquarters (*v.* 18). Ultimately though, the Beast and the ten horns (the Antichrist and his empire) will hate the prostitute and destroy her (*v.* 16).

Perhaps one of the most compelling pieces of information we have about the Harlot's identity is the name written on her forehead;

MYSTERY, BABYLON THE GREAT,
THE MOTHER OF HARLOTS
AND OF THE ABOMINATIONS
OF THE EARTH.
(Revelation 17:5, NKJV)

The Greek word for mystery, *mustérion,* can be defined as "a mystery or secret doctrine," particularly, "of which initiation is necessary."[4] "Mystery, Babylon the Great," could imply that this "new" religious system actually originates from the pagan practices of ancient Babylon, and *"Satan's so-called dark secrets"* (see Revelation 2:24). As King Solomon declared, *"What has been will be again, what has been done will be done again; there is nothing new under the sun,"*

(Ecclesiastes 1:9). And Solomon would know—being married to hundreds of foreign women would have given him a broad knowledge of world religions.

Interfaith Today

Propelled by rhetoric such as "reconciliation," "peace" and "acceptance," the interfaith movement is alive and well today. Since the year 2000, there have been a string of noteworthy developments towards this aim:

- The formation of the *World Council of Religious Leaders*, birthed out of the *United Nations Millennium World Peace Summit* in 2000. The WCRL aims to "...bring religious resources to support the work of the United Nations in our common quest for peace..."[5]
- The creation of "A Common Word Between Us and You," an open letter written by Muslim leaders to Christian leaders, with the aim of outlining commonalities between Islam, Christianity, and Judaism.[6]
- The subsequent initiative of *United Nations World Interfaith Harmony Week*.
- The *World Conference on Dialogue* held in Madrid in 2008, the brainchild of King Abdullah of Saudi Arabia.
- The founding of *King Abdullah Bin Abdulaziz International Center for Interreligious and Intercultural Dialogue*, in Vienna, 2012.
- The creation of the *Berlin Declaration on Interreligious Dialogue*, by the *European Council of Religious Leaders* in 2008, an interreligious council promoting cooperation between senior leaders of various faiths.[7]

We cannot know for certain what the end-time religious system will look like—whether it will be a synthesis of many religions, or a single religion taking precedence over others. In the later instance, one religion could function as an "umbrella institution," allowing other faiths to continue their religious practices as part of one entity. While we do not know for certain, we should heed any new developments that point towards a world religious system—if we miss the signs, we may be in danger of walking into deception. It is not enough to simply profess our faith—we must be rooted in unwavering conviction. If we do not stand firm in our faith, we will not stand at all (Isaiah 7:9).

Chapter 5

❖ ❖ ❖

Global Governance

B esides the Harlot, we encounter another imposing symbol in Revelation 17—the Beast. Fortunately for John (and us!), we are offered an angelic explanation of this outlandish creature:

"The beast, which you saw, once was, now is not, and yet will come up out of the Abyss and go to its destruction. The inhabitants of the earth whose names have not been written in the book of life from the creation of the world will be astonished when they see the beast, because it once was, now is not, and yet will come.

This calls for a mind with wisdom. The seven heads are seven hills on which the woman sits. They are also seven kings. Five have fallen, one is, the other has not yet come; but when he does come, he must remain for only a little while. The beast who once was, and now is not, is an eighth king. He belongs to the seven and is going to his destruction.

The ten horns you saw are ten kings who have not yet received a kingdom, but who for one hour will receive authority as kings along with the beast. They have one purpose and will give their power and authority to the beast.

They will wage war against the Lamb, but the Lamb will triumph over them because he is Lord of lords and King of kings—and with him will be his called, chosen and faithful followers." (Revelation 17: 8–14)

We learn that the Harlot and the Beast are two sides of the same coin. If the woman represents a false religious system, then the beast she rides represents the political aspect of the Antichrist's kingdom. Assuming that the "many waters" are under the beast's feet, this would indicate that the Antichrist's influence is far-reaching, over many nations and peoples. We are told that the seven hills or seven heads represent kings and their empires. As with other symbols in Revelation, this is not new; God uses a mountain to symbolize the kingdom of Babylon elsewhere in the Bible:

"I am against you, you destroying mountain, you who destroy the whole earth," declares the Lord. "I will stretch out my hand against you, roll you off the cliffs, and make you a burned-out mountain. (Jeremiah 51:25)

Throughout history, the antichrist spirit has tried many times to take complete dominion over the earth and destroy God's people. Every evil leader—from Haman, Antiochus Epiphanes, Nero, to Hitler—has served as a kind of "prototype" of the end-time Antichrist. To get an idea of who the Antichrist might *be*, we need to look back to who he might have *been*—the "original" Antichrist. Just as the seed of the Messiah can be traced back through the Davidic lineage to Abraham, so the Antichrist's spiritual lineage can be traced back to a single man. In Genesis, we read briefly of an impressive figure:

Cush was the father of Nimrod, who became a mighty warrior on the earth. He was a mighty hunter before the Lord;

that is why it is said, "Like Nimrod, a mighty hunter before the Lord." (Genesis 10:8–9)

Skilled in warfare and hunting, Nimrod was also the first ruler of the known world. His powerful influence was felt by all and could be seen in the cities and monumental buildings he erected (see Genesis 10:10–11). To discover what kind of man Nimrod was, it is important to note that the phrase *"before the Lord,"* in Genesis 10:8 does not denote that God endorsed Nimrod's actions—but rather, that Nimrod set himself against God; flagrantly rebelled in God's face.

The Jewish historian, Flavius Josephus, wrote of Nimrod:

> Now it was Nimrod who excited them to such an affront and contempt of God. He was the grandson of Ham, the son of Noah, a bold man, and of great strength of hand. He persuaded them not to ascribe it to God, as if it were through his means they were happy, but to believe that it was their own courage which procured that happiness. He also gradually changed the government into tyranny, seeing no other way of turning men from the fear of God, but to bring them into a constant dependence on his power. He also said he would be revenged on God, if he should have a mind to drown the world again; for that he would build a tower too high for the waters to reach. And that he would avenge himself on God for destroying their forefathers.[8]

If the tyrannical leader's desire to set himself against God and elevate himself to the heavens sounds vaguely familiar, that's because Nimrod was not the first to have such ambitions:

> You said in your heart, "I will ascend to the heavens; I will raise my throne above the stars of God I will ascend above

41

the tops of the clouds; I will make myself like the Most High." (Isaiah 14:13–14)

This verse gives us a huge clue to solve the riddle of the beast. Could it be, that Nimrod, the one responsible for establishing Babylon as the first world centers, was driven by Satan himself? Could the Enemy have inspired Nimrod to build the Tower of Babel, a symbol of rebellion against God himself? I believe the answer is an emphatic yes. For this reason, the nimrodic spirit of Babylon is likely to be operating through the Beast—the one John described as having been upon the earth but *"was not"* in his day. It could very well be that in the last days, the Enemy will use the "template" of the ancient Babylonian Empire to unite the world once more for his rebellious cause.

The Beast is truly a nasty piece of work. This ruler and his government will be openly blasphemous, corrupt to the core. The Beast will exalt himself above God and be known for his sinfulness (symbolized by the color scarlet, see Isaiah 1:18). His system will soak up every "ism" that has ever been created like a sponge, to subvert God's governance. Humanism, capitalism, communism, and socialism—he will use them all for his gain. In this way, the Beast will win favor with many and a godless world will look to his government for guidance.

In the Not So Distant Future

The symbols found in Revelation can seem so bizarre to our modern understanding that it can be easy to emotionally disconnect from what we read. Consequently, there is the very real danger of seeing the events of Revelation as some far-off fantasy. Revelation is already being fulfilled before our eyes, however—we just need to know what we are looking at. There are, for example, already several entities in existence that could either prove to be forerunners of a global governmental system or may one day form part of it. Two of these organizations are among the most prominent on the world stage today.

The United Nations

Although the United Nations does not profess to be a governmental agency, many of its functions carry the hallmarks of governance. Perhaps most well-known for its humanitarian efforts, the UN also exerts great influence in world affairs. For this reason, it is important that Christians at least have a basic understanding of the organization's functions and aims, remaining aware of any UN resolutions that may hold end-time significance.

The UN is comprised of six main departments, or "organs"— the Security Council, the General Assembly, the Economic and Social Council, the Trusteeship Council, the International Court of Justice and the Secretariat.

The Security Council is primarily responsible for peacekeeping and consists of 15 member countries. Five of these members are permanent (China, France, Russia, the United Kingdom, and the United States), and ten are elected for two-year terms. Nine votes are required to make a decision, except in the event that one of the "Big Five" countries casts a veto. If a solution cannot be reached peaceably (e.g. by way of mediation), then the Security Council has the power to enforce its decisions—by imposing sanctions or deploying peace-keeping forces, for example.

The General Assembly (alternately known as a "parliament of nations") consists of 193 member states. Although a much larger body than the Security Council, the General Assembly is unable to make recommendations on matters pertaining to peace and security. Members are restricted to vote or reach a consensus on lesser issues. Proposals have been made, however, that all world laws be passed by a "world parliament," and that these laws be enforced by a "world court of justice." If successful, the creation of a world parliament would only stand to increase the UN's power, making it a democratic institution. Ultimately, the UN sees a world parliament as a stepping stone to realizing a one world government.[9]

The World Court, seated in Peace Palace in the Hague, settles international disputes, as well as overseeing a staggering number of programs and specialized agencies. In almost every corner of the world, you will find UN Offices, peacekeeping missions, aid workers, and envoys. What's more, virtually every major world sector has a UN agency assigned to it, for example: food and agriculture (FAO), sustainable development and energy (UNDP), aviation and travel (ICAO), education, the sciences and culture (UNESCO), health (WHO), money (IMF), communications (ITU), and population (UNFPA), to name just a few.

Lastly, the United Nations is of special interest because of its strong focus on world peace—an essential ingredient for unifying countries under a common banner. At a debate that was part of the UN's 70th Anniversary commemorative events, Secretary General Ban Ki-Moon encouraged the world to look to the United Nation charter as a firm foundation in tumultuous times.[10] Such a sentiment frames the United Nations as a beacon of hope to humanity.

The European Union

Another entity of interest is the European Union. The EU operates in a similar fashion to the United Nations, as a supranational organization. The main decision-making bodies of the EU are: The European Parliament, The Council of the EU and the European Commission. These bodies are supported by: The Court of Justice of the EU, The European Central Bank and The Court of Auditors—giving the EU a tremendous amount of political influence, particularly in finances and law making.

For the purposes of this discussion, we will be looking primarily at the physical, rather than the political structure of the EU. The EU is seated in buildings laden with symbolism; rich in biblical and ancient imagery. The Louise Weiss building that houses the European Parliament is a striking example—its circular design is reminiscent of a Babylonian ziggurat, the type of structure the Tower of Babel's architects would likely have used. Intriguingly, the top of the building has an intentionally half-finished appearance (fig. 1, page 46). It also bears an uncanny resemblance to the painting "The Tower of Babel" (fig. 2, page 46), and a 1992 EU poster bearing the slogan "Europe: Many Tongues, One Voice." The poster's artwork unmistakably depicts the Tower of Babel in the background. Whether this resemblance is intentional or not, the message it sends is clear. The EU aspires to unite individuals for a common cause, in effect "reversing" the division caused at Babel.

Another striking symbol used by the EU is a woman riding a bull. A statue of this motif stand outside the EU parliamentary building, and another outside the EU headquarters in Brussels, Belgium. Inspired by Greek mythology, the statues portray Europa, a Phoenician princess coveted by the god Zeus (fig. 3, page 46). The legend says that Zeus disguised himself as a bull and abducted Europa, swimming with her on his back to the island of Crete.

Although accounts vary concerning how Europe came to bear Europa's name, the woman riding a bull has become a symbol for Europe, appearing on various euro coins, such as the Greek two-euro coin (fig. 4, page 47). On the surface, the association seems fairly benign. But is there more to the motif than meets the eye? It is uncanny, for example, that Europa shares the same origins as history's most infamous queen, the wicked Jezebel. Both were pagan Phoenician princesses. While I am not trying to suggest that the woman riding the beast *is* Europe, it is striking that the European Union would use a symbol so reminiscent of this end-time symbol.

The fact that Europa is depicted riding a bull is significant. In ancient times, bulls were associated with many pagan figures, including the Egyptian god Apis, the Canaanite deity Molech (mentioned numerous times in the Bible) and Greek minotaurs.

Fig. 1. European
Parliamentary
Building in
Strasberg, France.
Image credit:
Bigstock Photo[11]

Fig. 2: Pieter
Bruegel the Elder,
The Tower of
Babel. Image credit:
Bigstock Photo[12]

Fig. 3. Detail of
a fresco found in
Pompeii, depicting
Europa and Zeus in
bull form.
Image credit:
Wikimedia
Commons[13]

Fig. 4. National side of the Greek two-euro coin. Image credit: Bigstock Photo[14]

Fig. 5. Bas-relief bull depicted on the Ishtar gate, Ancient Babylon, Iraq. Image credits: Bigstock Photo[15]

Fig. 6. Section of a frieze on the Pergamon altar, the Pergamon Museum, Berlin. Image credits: Bigstock Photo[16]

One of the earliest surviving works of literature, the Mesopotamian "Epic of Gilgamesh," features a "mythic bull of heaven." The patron deity of the city of Babylon was a bull god called Marduk (fig. 5, page 47), also known as *Bel* (Baal of the Bible). This false god's identity is none other than Beelzebub (the Biblical rendering of the Ugaritic *Baal Zbl*). That the bull is, in fact, Satan's chosen emblem is confirmed indirectly in the book of Revelation:

> To the angel of the church in Pergamum write: These are the words of him who has the sharp, double-edged sword. I know where you live—where Satan has his throne... (Revelation 2:12–13)

In John's day, Pergamum was important for two reasons. Located in what is now modern-day Turkey, the city was a major political center, where rulings affected the entire Asia Minor region. Pergamum was also the home of a massive temple to the "king" of the Greek gods. At the top of the "Great Altar of Zeus" stood his chosen symbol—you guessed it—a bull. From this information, we can conclude that the bull/beast are one. Both are Satan's preferred icons, and both have been associated with world government (the antichrist system).

If you visit Pergamum today, you will not find the surviving foundation of Zeus/Satan's temple. In 1930, it was transplanted some 1150 miles away, to the Pergamum Museum in Berlin (fig. 6, page 47). Three years later, Adolf Hitler began his rise to power. Satan had effectively shifted his "throne" to Germany, in preparation for one of the most brutal attacks on God's people in history.

Working Towards a Common Aim

While the United Nations and the European Union are two of the most prominent organizations embracing the themes of global unity and governance, there are many others that share these aims. As the end-time clock advances, we are likely to see increasing moves towards globalization.

The idea of uniting the world as one is certainly not a new one, but today it is becoming more and more evident. Take for example the strikingly named "One World" Trade Center, now standing in the place of the former World Trade Center. The name is strongly suggestive a one world system.

Lastly, although the United Nations and the European Union may not ultimately prove to be part of such a system, their evolution over time and structural reforms indicate that they may be, (at the very least) strong prototypes of what is to come.

Chapter 6

Signs in the Heavens

There will be signs in the sun and moon and stars...
(Luke 21:25)

A s a child, I remember marveling at this verse, trying to imagine
what signs in the heavens might look like. The idea seemed
distant and fantastical, like something out of a sci-fi movie. Nowadays,
however, less imagination is required. Spectacular signs are being
displayed, right in front of our eyes.

In 2013, the world watched in awe as a burst of incredible footage
flashed across our TV screens—we saw a blinding light streaking across
the sky, windows spontaneously exploding, and a million shards of broken
glass sparkling in the snow. We saw people cowering from the impact
of an invisible blast and heard the terrified exclamations in Russian. On
that freezing morning of February the 15th, a meteor weighing more than
the Eiffel Tower fell on Russia, releasing shock waves equal to the force
of 30 Hiroshima nuclear bombs.[17] When I saw the footage for the first
time, it was so surreal that I thought I was seeing a movie.

The Bible is clear that the last days will be marked by remarkable
astronomical occurrences, or, *"signs in the heavens."* Like huge neon
signs, these events will point to the last days. At the time of writing,
the world is witnessing one such event—a phenomenon that has quietly
been playing out its celestial drama in 2015–2016.

The Blood Moons

A lunar eclipse, or "blood moon," is caused when the earth passes between the moon and the sun, causing the earth's shadow to fall upon the moon. When some of the light from the sun manages to pass through the earth's atmosphere, it blocks out every color in the light spectrum, except red. This light is refracted, causing a red hue to be cast upon the moon's surface.

The apostle John's apocalyptic vision seems to speak of this phenomenon:

> I watched as he opened the sixth seal. There was a great earthquake. The sun turned black like sackcloth made of goat hair, the whole moon turned blood red, and the stars in the sky fell to earth, as figs drop from a fig tree when shaken by a strong wind. (Revelation 6:12–13)

When four lunar eclipses occur consecutively, they are known as a lunar tetrad. Not all tetrads are created equal, however. To discern specifically which tetrads could be of significance, we must firstly understand that God's prophetic timetable does not operate on the calendar most commonly used today—the Gregorian calendar. In Genesis, God established creation on the Hebrew calendar. When we look at prophecy through the lens of the Hebrew calendar, it suddenly comes alive in a whole new way. Two excellent books on the topic of the blood moons and their prophetic significance are, "Blood Moons: Decoding the Imminent Heavenly Signs,"[18] by Pastor Mark Blitz, and, "Four Blood Moons: Something Is About to Change,"[19] by Pastor John Hagee.

When we align the lunar eclipses with the Hebrew calendar, an astonishing pattern begins to emerge. Although tetrads have not been uncommon in the last millennium, it is comparatively rare for tetrads to coincide exactly with the dates of Jewish feasts. In the two millennia since Christ's death, there have been seven prophetic tetrads. The tetrad of 2015–2016 will be the eighth. Past prophetic tetrads tend to fall on or close to the dates of significant historical events, particularly ones that impact Israel.[20]

Tetrad dates ..... Events/years
162, 163AD .... Time of intense persecution at the hands of Roman emperor Marcus Aurelius, 162-163AD
795, 796 AD .... Charlemagne defeats Islam, 795-800AD
842,843 AD .... Muslims sack Rome 846 AD
860,861 AD .... The Battle of Lalakaon, 863 AD
1493, 1494 AD ... The Spanish Inquisition, 1492 AD

The dates and feasts of the 2014–2015 lunar tetrad are:

Passover	Feast of	Passover	Feast of
4/15/14	Tabernacles	4/4/15	Tabernacles
	10/8/14		9/28/15

The 2015–2016 tetrad has a characteristic that sets it apart from the others. Of the 8 prophetic tetrads, it is the only one to be followed by a Jubilee, the fiftieth year after seven Shemitah cycles. (We will be discussing the Shemitah in more detail later.)

Two significant events have occurred in Israel during Jubilee years in the past century. In 1917, October 31, the Australian Light Horsemen played a crucial role in liberating Jerusalem from 400 years of Ottoman Turk rule.[21] The following month, the Balfour Declaration was signed, with a view to establish a Jewish homeland. Consequently, Israel experienced restoration, and many Jews began to return. Fast forward to the next Jubilee year and you come to 1966–67. On June 8, during the Six-Day War, Israel captured Jerusalem, consolidated the Jewish nation.

Could the Blood Moons Predict the Time of Jesus' Coming?

Lamentably, there have been attempts to use the blood moons to predict the exact time of Jesus' return, something we are explicitly warned not to do:

> But of that day and hour no one knows, not even the angels of heaven, but My Father only...Therefore you also be ready, for the Son of Man is coming at an hour you do not expect. (Matthew 24:36, 44, NKJV)

Only time will reveal what events the blood moons could be foreshadowing. For the moment, I believe we are simply to take them as a sign of the times we live in and to stay alert, ready and watchful for any eventuality.

Chapter 7

———— ❖ ❖ ❖ ————

Disasters and Plagues

There will be famines and earthquakes in various places.
All these are the beginning of birth pains.
(Matthew 24:7–8)

Natural disasters and plagues are mentioned over thirty times in the book of Revelation, making them one of the most prominent end-time signs. Over the past decade, you would have doubtless seen the extensive coverage of a whole raft of disasters—the South Asian Tsunami, Hurricane Katrina, the 2010 Haiti Earthquake, Ebola, the Black Saturday Fires in Australia, the Fukushima Tsunami—to name only a few. If you have suspected that natural disasters are becoming more frequent, you are right.

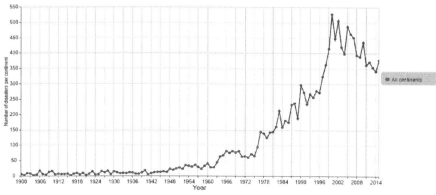

EM-DAT. The OFDA/CRED International Disaster Database - www.emdat.be - Université Catholique de Louvain, Brussels - Belgium

EM-DAT, The International Disaster Database, reports that the number of natural disasters has increased significantly from the turn of the 20th century to the present day. The number of disasters recorded in 1900 was 6. By the year 2000, it had risen to 527.[22]

The Bible makes mention of all imaginable natural, man-made, and biological catastrophes, including earthquakes (see Mark 13:8, Revelation 16:18), tsunamis (Luke 21:25), hailstorms (Revelation 16:21), famines (Luke 21:11), and even tornados (also called "whirlwinds," in Isaiah 40:24). Revelation speaks of catastrophes capable of wiping out up to a third of the earth's total population—something that would have been incomprehensible in John's day:

> I looked, and there before me was a pale horse! Its rider was named Death, and Hades was following close behind him. They were given power over a fourth of the earth to kill by sword, famine and plague, and by the wild beasts of the earth. (Revelation 6:8)
>
> The horses and riders I saw in my vision looked like this: Their breastplates were fiery red, dark blue, and yellow as sulfur. The heads of the horses resembled the heads of lions, and out of their mouths came fire, smoke and sulfur. A third of mankind was killed by the three plagues of fire, smoke and sulfur that came out of their mouths. (Revelation 9:17–18)

To put these figures into perspective, approximately 2.4% of the world's population was killed during the Second World War.[23] The only catastrophe that has come close to killing a third of the world's population was the bubonic plague outbreak in the 14th century.

The reference in Revelation 6:8 to people being killed by wild beasts seems almost archaic to us today. With the advance of modern technology, man has invented ways to overcome attacks from just about any animal; we have invented electronic shark deterrents, snake antivenoms, and hunting rifles. There remains, however, one threat that man has not been able to completely eradicate—disease. Zoonoses are diseases originating from animals that can be transmitted to humans. The bubonic plague that caused the Black Death is an example of a zoonosis. The outbreak was caused when the bacteria Yersinia pestis was transmitted from rats and fleas to humans. Over the past 25 years, the world has seen an increase in the variety and frequency of zoonosis epidemics, with the emergence of diseases such as avian influenza (H5N1), swine flu (H1N1), Ebola (thought to have originated from bats), and the recent Zika virus, carried by mosquitoes.[24] These in mind, suddenly the idea of *"wild beasts"* decimating a quarter of the world's population does not seem like such a far-fetched idea.

While there are a number of factors contributing to the spread of zoonoses (such as increased travel by air), there are two of particular concern.

The first is genetic modification—a practice that is fast becoming commonplace, even as experimentation becomes more outlandish. Take, for example, the recent experiments injecting human brain cells into mice to enhance their intelligence or the creation of human-animal hybrids (known as "chimeras").[25] In 2015, reports emerged of 150 chimeras that were secretly grown in laboratories in the United Kingdom. Allegedly created for discovering cures for diseases, the embryos were prohibited from developing past 14 days and were destroyed.[26] In the United States, the National Health Institute announced that they planned to lift a ban on funding research involving injecting human stem cells into animal embryos.[27] Surely such unnatural tinkering with nature is not without consequences. If any scenario would be likely to open a pandora's box of zoonoses, this would be it.

The second factor increasing the likelihood of zoonoses is their potential use in biological warfare.[28] The anthrax scare of 2001 gave us a glimpse into the capabilities of this type of warfare (anthrax originated from farm animals). The vast majority of pathogens used for bioterrorism are zoonoses.

Nuclear Warfare

Another significant type of disaster that did not exist in John's day—nuclear warfare—has become of major global concern. It is possible that the Bible also speaks of this particular kind of disaster:

> This is the plague with which the Lord will strike all the nations that fought against Jerusalem: Their flesh will rot while they are still standing on their feet, their eyes will rot in their sockets, and their tongues will rot in their mouths. (Zechariah 14:12)

There is a weapon in existence today that is capable causing the devastation described in this verse. The effects of a neutron bomb, or Enhanced Radiation Weapon, are virtually identical:

> "The neutron bomb delivers blast and heat effects that are confined to an area of only a few hundred yards in radius. But within a somewhat larger area it throws off a massive wave of neutron and gamma radiation, which can penetrate armor or several feet of earth. *This radiation is extremely destructive to living tissue.*"[29] (emphasis added)

Revelation on the Radar

As we see the changes taking place around us, let us avoid the tendency to view scientific and technological developments, natural disasters, and the media in isolation. Rather, let us view them through the lens of prophecy and the Word, understanding their relationship with one another and how they correlate.

Over the last few years, for example, Hollywood has released a barrage of disaster movies. While I would certainly never advocate using a movie to interpret the Word, it is worth noting that many movies are increasingly depicting apocalyptic scenarios. It could very well be that God is using Hollywood to warn the world of what is to come.

Above all, we must stay connected with the heart of God, listening to His voice and walking closely with Him in an increasingly unstable world. We will be discussing ways to maintain a strong relationship with the Father a little later.

Chapter 8

❖ ❖ ❖

The Mark

For millennia, people have wondered about the enigmatic "mark of the Beast." What will it look like? How will it be applied? And how will we know it is the mark? As is the case with many end-time signs, we have new clues available to us today to help unlock the mystery. Technology may hold the answer.

The implantable microchip has long been seen as a possible candidate for the mark of the Beast by many modern believers. Radio Frequency Identification (RFID) chips are tiny enough to be implanted into the human body. They can be used for financial transactions, a key characteristic of the mark of the Beast (see Revelation 13:17). RFID chips are being used today for economic and identification purposes—in contactless applications, for example, such as Pay Pass, tap and pay credit cards, and e-passports. The chips have a wide range of other uses you are likely to have encountered. If you are a library user, you may have used RFID technology to check out your books, or you may have come across microchip technology implanted in merchandise (fast becoming a way of keeping track of product inventory). If you own a pet, the chances are that they are microchipped.

While it might *seem* like a huge leap to imagine chips transitioning from our bank cards to our bodies, this is already happening. In 2004, the United States Food and Drug Administration (FDA) approved the

RFID chip for human use.[30] There are already numerous cases of people being implanted with a chip. A night club in Barcelona, for example, gives club-goers the option of being implanted with a RFID chip. The chip acts as a membership card and enables them to make purchases at the bar.[31] In August 2014, Ben Slater joined a small but growing number of Australians receiving a microchip.[32] The digital advertising director chose to be implanted with a RFID chip, in the anticipation that smartphones will one day read the chips.[33]

At Epicenter, a high-tech office block in Sweden, biohacking[34] company BioNyfken has rolled out the technology, enabling their employees to open doors, use photocopiers and perform other office tasks simply by swiping a chip implanted in their hand. Chief "disruption officer," Hannes Sjoblad, gives a startling insight into the microchips potential:

> "We want to be able to understand this technology before big corporates and big government come to us and say everyone should get chipped—the tax authority chip, the Google or Facebook chip."[35]

While receiving a chip is, of course, voluntary at present, a day is foreseeable when it could be mandatory. Society is already being conditioned to feel safe with the technology. Claims have been made, for example, that the chip can protect against identity theft– "You'll never lose the chip, and it makes physical theft impossible."[36] In 2008, the chip's medical application was promoted in a commercial for Verichip (now PositiveID), stating that the chip could; "connect you [and]be with you, when every second counts in the emergency room," and could help people who forget to take their medications.[37] The psychology is subtle but powerful, as familiar as the fear tactics used in insurance commercials. It is insinuated that the individual who does not have a chip is placing themselves at risk, particularly in an emergency scenario. So far, this kind of marketing seems to be having a measure of success.

In 2004, a group of over 1000 Mexicans and 160 government officials pioneered the technology and were implanted with a chip.[38] The number of people being implanted with a chip worldwide is steadily growing.

Red Flags

Viewed through Scripture, it is easy to see how the microchip has been associated with the mark of the Beast:

[The beast] also forced all people, great and small, rich and poor, free and slave, to receive a mark on their right hands or on their foreheads, so that they could not buy or sell unless they had the mark, which is the name of the beast or the number of its name. This calls for wisdom. Let the person who has insight calculate the number of the beast, for it is the number of a man. That number is 666. (Revelation 13:16–18)

From these verses, we learn that the mark of the Beast is:

1) **A physical, permanent mark people will receive on their bodies.**
The Greek word used in this instance is *charagma*, meaning "sculpture, engraving, a stamp, sign."[39] Charagma was originally used to refer to an impress on a coin or seal.

2) **Received on people's hands or foreheads.**
The RFID chip is usually implanted in the hand, specifically between the thumb and index finger. While RFID chips are rarely implanted in the forehead, one of RFID's latest incarnations may make this possible (the technology is constantly evolving). A recent ground-breaking development means that a chip may not even be necessary for RFID transmissions. Invisible RFID ink is biocompatible, does not

contain any metals and can be transparent or colored. It is applied in 5–10 seconds by a "stamp or tattoo" and has been deemed safe for cattle and people.[40] As well as being used to track livestock, it is hoped that in the future the technology will be used to protect military personnel.[41] The mark can be placed anywhere on the body.

3) **Used for economic purposes.**

Charagma has economic connotations, referring to a coin being stamped. While the chip's current economic applications may or may not point to *the* actual Charagma, society is certainly being familiarized with the idea of using a type of electronic "tag" for transactions. It has long been common knowledge in the financial sector that the world is ultimately headed towards a cashless society. In an interview with Ben Slater, The Sydney Morning Herald reported: "It is thought that implantable microchips, if they were to ever become popular in use, would form a part of the cashless society."[42]

4) **Tied to Identification.**

Charagma is also an "identification marker, a physical brand," showing ownership—such as the mark slaves were forced to receive by their Roman masters. In contrast, the mark of the Beast is received by an individual *consenting* to become part of the Antichrist's system, effectively becoming his property. Like an electronic fingerprint, each microchip has a unique sixteen-digit number encryption that can be used for identification purposes.

A False Alarm?

At this point, you may well be thinking—"what if the mark of the Beast is *not* a chip or any form of RFID?" It may not be. There is, of course, the possibility that the mark could be something else entirely.

One alternative theory suggests that the mark could be a figurative, rather than a literal mark. Just as Christians receive the invisible seal of the Holy Spirit, so those who give themselves over to worshipping the Beast could receive a kind of demonic seal—an "unholy spirit." Whether the mark proves to be literal or spiritual, however, what is paramount is that we understand what it *signifies*.

If we find ourselves one day confronted with the mark, we will recognize it by its unmistakable association with the Beast and his system. Some have wondered if it would be possible to accidentally accept the mark of the Beast. The Word tells us though, that the mark is inextricably tied to worship:

> "If anyone worships the beast and its image and receives its mark on their forehead or on their hand." (Revelation 14:9)

Receiving the mark is not just a sign of assimilation into the Beast's kingdom, it is a sign of complete devotion and alliance. At this time, there is not yet a universal mark people can receive that is explicitly and emphatically tied to worshipping the Antichrist. That being said, I would certainly not recommend receiving any kind of foreign mark or implant, even if it simply proves to be a prototype of the mark to come.

❖ ❖ ❖

Chapter 9

Economic Meltdowns

Of all the recent end-time signs, perhaps the most widely felt was the Global Financial Crisis of 2008. The Word is not silent on the topic of financial collapses—scarcity, lack, and failing production are all signs of the last days.

Alas for that day! For the day of the Lord is near; it will come like destruction from the Almighty. Has not the food been cut off before our very eyes—joy and gladness from the house of our God? The seeds are shriveled beneath the clods. The storehouses are in ruins, the granaries have been broken down, for the grain has dried up. (Joel 1:15–17)

Revelation speaks of a time of great inflation:

When the Lamb opened the third seal, I heard the third living creature say, "Come!" I looked, and there before me was a black horse! Its rider was holding a pair of scales in his hand. Then I heard what sounded like a voice among the four living creatures, saying, "Two pounds of wheat for a day's wages, and six pounds of barley for a day's wages, and do not damage the oil and the wine! (Revelation 6:5–6)

The causes of these financial dire straits are revealed in the book of James:

> Now listen, you rich people, weep and wail because of the misery that is coming on you. Your wealth has rotted, and moths have eaten your clothes. Your gold and silver are corroded. Their corrosion will testify against you and eat your flesh like fire. You have hoarded wealth *in the last days*... You have lived on earth in luxury and self-indulgence. (James 5:1–3,5, emphasis added)

Today most analysts agree with this diagnosis, attributing the Global Financial Crisis of 2008 to greed, a burgeoning national debt, and to unbridled spending.

The Shemitah

Astonishingly, the Word reveals that the rise and fall of economic systems follows a unique template. To understand the *prophetic* dimensions of financial crashes, we must look firstly to the *economic* dynamics God has established on earth. Tucked away in Deuteronomy, we find a set of principles that still influence the financial realm today. The *Shemitah*, or "release," reveals a biblical pattern affecting economic cycles:

> At the end of every seven years you must cancel debts. This is how it is to be done: Every creditor shall cancel any loan they have made to a fellow Israelite. They shall not require payment from anyone among their own people, because the Lord's time for canceling debts has been proclaimed. You may require payment from a foreigner, but you must cancel any debt your fellow Israelite owes you. However, there need be no poor people among you, for in the land the Lord your God is giving you to possess as your inheritance, he will

richly bless you, if only you fully obey the Lord your God and are careful to follow all these commands I am giving you today. For the Lord your God will bless you as he has promised, and you will lend to many nations but will borrow from none. You will rule over many nations but none will rule over you. (Deuteronomy 15:1–6)

The Shemitah pattern of debt cancellation demonstrates God's compassion for those unable to pay their debts, and speaks of His wisdom for personal and national finances. When an economy is governed by the Shemitah, debt cannot accumulate indefinitely. When the Shemitah is disregarded (i.e. when a debt-based economy is in place), repercussions are felt in the financial and agricultural realms. For a comprehensive explanation of the Shemitah, the book "The Mystery of the Shemitah," by Messianic Rabbi Jonathan Cahn, is a wonderful reference.[43]

The Dynamics of the Shemitah

The Shemitah has three key dynamics. The first is *timing*. The Shemitah is governed by the Hebraic calendar. Unlike Gregorian chronology, the Jewish year does not begin after the 12th month. It commences in the month of Tishri, the seventh month of the Jewish calendar. Tishri runs between September–October. The last month of the Hebrew year is Elul, falling between August–September. The final day of the Jewish year is Elul 29th. A Sabbath year culminates on this day with the remission (or "wiping away") of debts.

The second dynamic of the Shemitah is *obedience*. In accordance with the principle of reaping and sowing, God has set before His people positive and negative consequences for honoring or dishonoring the Shemitah. As is the case with most biblical precepts, the primary purpose of the Shemitah is to *protect*. In the same way that the command "do not commit adultery" is designed to protect and guard marriage, the Shemitah is designed to protect God's people from poverty and bondage to debt.

The Word outlines the financial consequences of obeying and disobeying God's economic principles:

Blessings of obedience	Curses of disobedience
"There should be no poor among you" (Deut. 15:4)*	Nothing will prosper (Deut. 28:17–18)
"The Lord your God will richly bless you" (Deut. 15:4)	Scarcity, theft, financial hardship, lack. Unable to enjoy the fruit of your labor (Deut. 28:30–31)
"The land will yield its fruit." (Lev. 25:19)	"Your soil will not yield its crops nor will the trees of the land yield their fruit." Failing agricultural production. (Lev. 26:20)
"You will lend to other nations" (Deut. 15:6)	Need to borrow from other nations, in debt to them (Deut. 28:44)
"I will settle you in your own land" (Ezek. 37:14)	Building houses but not being able to live in them, i.e. foreclosures. (Deut. 28:30)

* blessings/curses found in Deuteronomy 15 are directly associated with the Shemitah.

The third dynamic of the Shemitah is *trust*. Principles such as the Shemitah and tithing test our faith in God to meet our needs. Each time the Israelites canceled debts and allowed their fields to become fallow for a year (see Leviticus 25:1–7), they were in effect saying, "God I trust you with my finances—they are not built on debt, but on Your provision. I trust that you will multiply my produce threefold and that I will have all that I need to get me through to the next harvest."

When the Bottom Falls Out

When the values of the Shemitah are discarded, what "goes up" literally "comes down." The market crash of 2008 was caused by a frenzy of subprime mortgages, easy lending, and debt-financed consumer spending, leaving trillions of dollars of national debt in its wake. For the nation living beyond its means, rejecting God's principles, the Shemitah can signal economic collapse or disaster.

When we look at the incidents of catastrophic market crashes in the past, a remarkable pattern begins to emerge. Many significant financial calamities have taken place in Shemitah years. This "Shemitah-pattern" can be seen throughout the 20th Century and up to the present day.[44]

Financial Crisis/causes	Gregorian Years	Shemitah Year
Severe drought, resulting in low food supply	1901-1903	5663
Start of the Great Depression	1930-32	5691
Beginning of early 1980's recession	1979-80	5740
Black Monday crisis	1986-87	5747
Bond Market Massacre	1994	5754

The last two economic crashes have been so precise in their timing that they have fallen, not just on a Shemitah year, but on the exact day of remission, the day assigned for the wiping away of debts.

Event	Gregorian Date	Jewish Date	Effects
Post 9/11 stock market crash	29 September 2001	29 Elul, 5761	Greatest stock market crash in history at the time, the market fell by 648 points.
2008 GFC	29 September 2008	29 Elul, 5768	Greatest stock market crash to date, market fell by 777 points

The Shemitah of 2008 has an exceptional feature, not seen in any of the previous crashes—a phenomenon that has been called the "Mystery of Sevens."[45] The crash took place in the seventh month of the seventh year. The stock market fell a record 777 points, after the rejection of a government bailout for 700 billion. In the case of the 2008 *and* 2001 crashes, 7% of Wall Street was wiped out.

Shemitah Now

The Shemitah of September 2015–September 2016 (the Hebrew year 5776), also exhibits an unusual feature. Every 49 years (a period of seven sevens) a Jubilee year falls (see Leviticus 25:8–13). Some scholars believe that the year 5776 was the 49th year of the Jubilee cycle. According to this theory, the Shemitah year of 5776 would be followed by a Jubilee year. The Jubilee of 5777 (2016-2017) would be the 70th since Israel came out of Egypt, and the 40th since Christ's death and resurrection.

It is worth noting here that the Shemitah does not always bring economic disaster. In some instances, calamity comes in different forms—such as natural disasters. Some have speculated that the Jubilee of 5777 could bring a significant event for the nation of Israel. Only history, however, will reveal with certainty the events the Jubilee may be heralding.

More importantly, we must understand that God is not bound by man's predictions, only by His Word. God chooses when and how He brings signs to pass. Man's predictions may stand or fall, but God's Word will never pass away.

❖ ❖ ❖

Chapter 10

A Moral Slippery Slope
and the Coming Persecution

In a 2015 Gallup Values and Beliefs poll, 72% of Americans said that the state of moral values in the US was getting worse rather than better, compared to 67% in 2002.[46] The poll also showed a strong upward trend in the acceptability of a number of moral issues. Since the early 2000s, Americans are more likely to find reproductive issues such as abortion and cloning acceptable. The strongest trends of acceptability were sex between an unmarried woman and man (supported by 68% of Americans), homosexual relations (63%) and divorce (71%). Furthermore, seven in ten Americans now back doctor-assisted suicide.[47] Morality has also been declining globally. Acts of terrorism[48] and crimes such as human trafficking (particularly trafficking children)[49] have increased significantly, with drug-related crimes most on the rise.[50]

Whilst these trends may sound alarming, they should come as no surprise to us. The apostle Paul warned us of such decay, his words echoing down to our present day:

But mark this: There will be terrible times in the last days. People will be lovers of themselves, lovers of money, boastful, proud, abusive, disobedient to their parents, ungrateful, unholy, without love, unforgiving, slanderous, without self-control, brutal, not lovers of the good, treacherous, rash, conceited, lovers of pleasure rather than lovers of God—having a form of godliness but denying its power. (2 Timothy 3:1–5)

Sadly, this passage reveals that moral decay not limited to the world. In the last days, there will also be *believers* who are lovers of themselves, lovers of money, proud, etc.—having a form of "godliness," that lacks the true power of God. When we see such unrighteousness flourish, we can be sure that we are living in the times Jesus spoke of, when *"iniquity [will] abound"* (see Matthew 24:12).

Rising Persecution

...you will be hated by all nations for my name's sake. (Matthew 24:9)

Another sign of the last days is an increase in Christian persecution. As quickly as prayer is removed from schools and the Ten Commandments are torn down from courthouses, anti-Christian sentiment and hostility toward godly values are on the rise. In other words, when society tries to remove God, it creates a vacuum that persecution thrives in.

In contrast to the physical beatings and threats believers often face in countries traditionally hostile to the gospel, Western persecution tends to be characterized by social and political intimidation. The "agent" paving the way for rising persecution in the West is undoubtedly the spirit of political correctness. Not content to rule secular society, this spirit attempts to infiltrate the church, eroding the foundation with compromise and apathy.

To effectively stand against this spirit, we must recognize it for what it is—an antichrist spirit, intent on calling "evil good, and good evil" (Isaiah 5:20). The "war-cry" of political correctness is "freedom!"—

freedom from God's laws, freedom from accountability to a Supreme Being, freedom to follow one's own moral convictions and freedom to follow the tenets of humanism, unhindered. Humanism—basically, "man-as-god," is a concept we will be exploring in more detail.

On the War Path

Those who embrace political correctness claim that it upholds values such as tolerance, acceptance, and freedom of speech. This is only partially true, however—political correctness *does* uphold freedom of speech, but usually only for one party. Liberal ideologies are often praised and encouraged, while those upholding God's standards are met with aggression. Not content to simply express opinions, political correctness actively seeks shut down opinions to the contrary—often in violation of religious freedom.

Shortly after homosexual marriage was legalized in the United States, Franklin Graham warned, "You better be ready and you better be prepared because it's coming. There will be persecution of Christians for our stand."[51] Less than two months afterward, there were already several cases of intimidation against Christians. Christian bakers who declined to bake cakes for same-sex weddings were forced to close their businesses after receiving hefty fines[52] and military personnel were stood down from their positions, after voicing their convictions on homosexuality.[53]

One of the most publicized of these early cases was that of Kim Davis, the Kentucky county clerk jailed for refusing to issue marriage licenses to homosexual couples. Not willing to allow Kim Davis to exercise freedom of conscience, those who opposed her leveled a barrage of deeply personal affronts and vicious attacks. One group of activists placed billboards mocking Davis in her hometown.[54] Whether you agree or disagree with Davis' decision to put her convictions before the duties of her office, one thing is certain—she was jailed as the direct result of her Christian beliefs.

Davis' case and others like it raise questions, such as: "Will it remain possible for Christians to hold positions of authority and public office?" and, "will everyday business owners be able to maintain their stance *and* retain their jobs?" These are some of the dilemmas believers face as they decide whether or not to make a stand.

The issue of religious freedom is certainly not restricted to government sectors. The American educational sector, once founded on Christian institutions, is now rife with anti-Christian sentiment. In 2013, University student Ryan Rotela was ordered not to return to class after he refused to turn in a paper. The "assignment," set by Rotela's intercultural communications professor, was to write the name of Jesus on a piece of paper and stomp on it.[55] In the medical field, the spirit of political correctness seeks to ban Christians from wearing crosses at work, and doctors from praying with patients.[56]

Strength in Times of Persecution

So how then should we live? I believe that while we should love and warn those who disregard God's laws, we need to understand that sin *will* abound in the last days (see Matthew 24:12). We must exercise discernment, understanding that now, more than ever before, the Enemy seeks to wage war on God's children. We can take heart—secure in the knowledge that although the darkness will try and snuff out the light for a little longer, ultimately the light will never be overcome—"the light shines in the darkness, and the darkness has not overcome it" (John 1:5).

Shaking Felt on Our Knees

Several years ago, during my prayer time, God spoke to me:

"The state of the world today is like an earthquake about to happen. Before the earthquake will come small tremors. These tremors will not be felt by those engrossed in the cares of the world. Only those who are always before me, those who live in a constant attitude of prayer, with their hands and knees pressed to the ground—those in tune with

my Spirit—will feel and recognize the 'vibrations' before the major shaking that is to come."

Now is the time to make a commitment to live in holiness, no matter the cost. It is the time to discern, with open ears and hearts, what the Spirit is saying—in our personal walks with the Lord and through His servants the prophets. Later, we will be looking at the ways we can prepare ourselves, both spiritually and practically, for the days ahead.

PART THREE:

Avoiding Deception

Chapter 11

Blurred Gospels

...The love of most will grow cold.
(Matthew 24:12)

As the world experiences intense upheaval, the church is also experiencing a shift. Across the globe, there is a polarization taking place among believers, of hot and cold. We find ourselves rapidly passing the era of lukewarm Christianity—moving into a season that demands either scalding conviction or icy indifference of us. None of us should believe that we are immune to grow cold in the faith. We need to be keenly aware of the strategies the Enemy would use to destabilize our convictions.

One Word, Many Gospels

Of all the Enemy's tactics, Satan's "weapon of choice" is to try and undermine the Word. This is the oldest of his oldest strategies, dating back to the garden of Eden. The Enemy does not use an outright lie to begin with, he uses the Word as a starting point and then "blurs" it, until it becomes a half-truth. Unfortunately, this "blurring" has crept into much of today's preaching, creating a relative smorgasbord of gospel variations. Using subtle distortions, the enemy has succeeded in proliferating many versions of the true Word.

"Blurred gospels" can be so hard to detect because of the

seed of truth they contain. They are built around powerful, very real revelations, wrapped up in Scriptures that have been taken out of context or misrepresented. In this way, a biblical truth becomes a counterfeit teaching. When people flock to hear such false doctrines, we can be sure that we are living in the last days:

> For the time will come when people will not put up with sound doctrine. Instead, to suit their own desires, they will gather around them a great number of teachers to say what their itching ears want to hear. (2 Timothy 4:3)

Being able to recognize false doctrine is half the fight, in the battle to guard our hearts. In this section, we will look at some popular teaching that has taken hold in the church today.

In Search of the Truth

Two things should be noted before we begin our discussion—firstly, that it will not be comprehensive, by any means. I have narrowed the raft of "blurred gospels" down to four. Most false teaching can fall under one of these four categories.

Secondly, I will be applying the principle of "holding the truth in tension."[57]

This is the idea that all biblical truths can be stretched to polar extremes, and that somewhere in the middle lies the "balanced truth."

This analysis is not intended to condemn, but to cause believers to really question *what* they believe and *why* they believe it. More than ever, it is time for us to examine our hearts and ensure we are "believing right."

❖ ❖ ❖

Chapter 12

Humanism:
The "Man-made" Gospel

The Dawn of Humanism

"That's not Jesus!" That's a hologram!" For a long time, the man's words in my dream continued to puzzle me. The reference seemed so bizarre, so out of place. Why a hologram? One day, when I was least expecting it, God unveiled the mystery. He showed me that the man had attributed Jesus' supernatural presence in the room to a physical, man-made phenomenon—an empty one at that. His attempt to explain away God with his human logic represents our first "blurred gospel."

Humanism is an ideology that puts man's thoughts and ways above God's, attempting to replace the supernatural with all man's "-ologies." To understand how this doctrine has made inroads into the church today, we must look back to its origins.

Humanism has been around since the garden of Eden. It was conceived when the Enemy offered Adam and Eve the chance to become "gods" (that is, the masters of their own destinies), by eating from the Tree of the Knowledge of Good and Evil. Interestingly, it was not just the fruit's physical appearance that seduced Eve, but the suggestion that it could make her "wise."

When the woman saw that the fruit of the tree was good for food and pleasing to the eye, and also desirable for gaining wisdom, she took some and ate it..." (Genesis 3:6)

The theme of obtaining "higher knowledge" persisted throughout the ages, rising to prominence in the Enlightenment. The idea of enlightenment is central to many human philosophies and religions—Buddhism and the New Age, for example. The quest for enlightened knowledge also forms the basis of most, if not all secret societies.

Modern humanism was birthed in ancient Greece, in a society obsessed with the human form and intellect. This obsession is nowhere more evident than in the sculptures and art created by the ancient Greeks, depicting the human body with ideal proportions and muscularity. The Olympic Games stand testament to the Greeks worship of athleticism—a mania that continues today in our sports-mad society. They also laid the foundation for modern politics, with the creation of democracy. Disciplines such as philosophy and psychology emerged, as the sciences and arts came into their own. The apostle Paul encountered Greek humanism when he debated the Epicurean and Stoic philosophers in Athens (see Acts 17:16–34).

Greek and Roman ideals enjoyed a revival during the Renaissance, but it wasn't until the French Revolution that humanism was institutionalized as the *Culte de la Raison* (Cult of Reason.) During this era, Notre-Dame Cathedral became known as the *Temple de la Raison* (Temple to Reason), and a small Greek temple was erected inside, containing an "Altar to Reason." A ritual "Feast of Reason" was instituted, with participants paying homage to a woman dressed as "Lady Liberty." Based on the Roman goddess "Libertas," she became the figurehead of the French Revolution, replacing the Virgin Mary on some altars for a time. This very same Lady Liberty—the personification of "enlightenment" and humanistic "freedom"—is represented in the statue given to the United States by France in 1886. In fact, the Statue of Liberty's full title is *La Liberté Éclairant le Monde* (Liberty

Enlightening the World).

The founding of the "First Humanist Society of New York" in 1929 established modern Humanism. In 1933, humanist beliefs were explicitly outlined for the first time in writing, in Humanist Manifesto I. Two successor documents have since been written, Humanist Manifesto II (1973) and Humanist Manifesto III (2003). While versions II and III of the manifestos have an atheistic tone, version I makes provisions for "religious" humanism. In the same way that the ancient Greeks saw humanism as being compatible with worshipping their gods, Humanist Manifesto I encompasses spirituality and religious practices, maintaining that:

- The highest pursuit of a human being is the development, fulfillment, and complete realization of their own personality. This occurs in the temporal, rather than the eternal—in living for the moment.
- "Religious emotions" should be found in a "heightened sense of personal life and in a cooperative effort to promote social well-being,"[58] rather than in prayer and worship.
- Associations and institutions exist for the fulfillment and enhancement of human life.
- Religious rituals exist for human fulfillment.

I Just Want to be Happy

I have a soft spot for bridal programs. When I want to relax and put up my feet, I turn on the lifestyle channels and look for swathes of white satin. There is something beautiful and uplifting about seeing a bride-to-be's joy when she finds the gown of her dreams, the most important dress she will ever wear. At the beginning of the segment, each bride and groom-to-be are asked some questions—how did you meet, what attracted you to him/her? etc. I began to notice that the same answers would come up, time and again—"We're so compatible...I love how I feel when I am with him...he understands me...she completes me." Inevitably the phrase, "he/she makes me so happy," was said. That got me thinking. How much humanism (me-centered thinking) has crept into the way we view relationships? How much have relationships become about what another person can offer us? I think forward for a moment to what these couple's marriages may look like. How will they survive if (and when) the day comes when their spouse no longer makes them happy?

Humanism has convinced society that love is based on happiness and personal fulfillment. Ultimately though, this type of love rarely stands the test of hardships. It tends not to make allowances for other's weaknesses and for painful processes. Everyday challenges and sorrows are simply not part of the romantic picture Hollywood paints. Sadly, this is the very sort of thinking that has infiltrated the church, affecting the way that many of us see our relationship with God. We have been led to believe that God's love for us is measured by the absence of trials. If our lives are filled with blessings and ease, then God's favor must shine upon us. If we encounter suffering, then He must have turned His face from us.

Dear Friend, let us not fall for the lie that God is more concerned more with our undivided happiness than our ongoing character development and sanctification. A Christian walk built primarily on happiness is like an ornamental tree with a shallow root system, planted in sand—its fruit provides no nourishment, and, if it were pulled out by the trunk, it would be easily uprooted. If our relationship with God revolves around what He can do for us (i.e. get us out of problems, give us a better life, take away all suffering, make us happy, etc.) then we are at risk falling away when times get tough. To test yourself in this area, think about how you react when faced with hardship. Humanism says "I must do everything in my power to make myself happy again. I must do all I can to get out of this situation." The Word says, *"I will trust in the Lord with all my heart and lean not on my own understanding... I have learned the secret of being content in any and every situation—I can do all things through Christ who strengthens me"* (Proverbs 3:5,

Philippians 4:12,13).

Humanism in the Church

Humanism is the enemy of God-centered worship—it aims to place "man-god" at the center of our lives, rather than God Almighty. Humanism's "religious emotions" are expressed through self-realization, and a heightened sense of personal life—as opposed to a *surrendered* life.

Humanism in the church can often be identified by an over-abundance of programs, courses, meetings and social activities directed primarily at promoting self-esteem and well-being. Discipleship is often to the end of creating *fulfilled* individuals, capable of performing effective Christian service, rather than creating *worshippers*. While I am not trying to suggest that church programs and activities are inherently wrong, they should be God-focused, not us-focused. The latter can actually keep us in a state of spiritual infancy, rather than producing growth.

As well as encouraging the believer to be happy and fulfilled, humanism exalts self-reliance, encouraging the Christian to believe he or she is ultimately in charge of his/her life. Such theology relegates God to the level of an employee. The truth is, that although God's plans and purposes are sovereign, He lovingly invites us to be part of what He is doing. He allows us the privilege of being His co-workers (see 1 Corinthians 3:9, 2 Corinthians 6:1).

If you need further proof of "Christian" humanism's self-centered focus, I encourage you to do the following exercise, next time you are in a Christian bookstore: scan through the titles on the shelves, particularly in the "Christian Living" section. Now, take note of how many of those titles contain the words "I," "you" or "your?" How many imply that you, through implementing some sort of behavioral change, can be personally empowered? How many books advocate psychological, rather than *supernatural* transformation?

A couple of years ago, at my local Christian bookstore, my eyes were opened to the sheer number of Christian books that would be perfectly at home in the motivational or self-help section of a public library. Since Dr. Norman Peale wrote "The Power of Positive Thinking" in 1952, scores of books have been written about how to transform ourselves and/or others, and be more happy, successful and fulfilled. Not limited to Christian books, these themes also resonate loudly in the lyrics of many self-centric Christian worship songs.

The idea that we can bring about self-transformation is not a new one. Transcendentalism, birthed in America in the 1820's, is a philosophical movement based on the belief that humans are essentially good, and that self-reliance and independence lead to greater morality—a belief that is totally at odds with the Word: *"For I know that nothing good dwells in me, that is, in my flesh. For I have the desire to do what is right, but not the ability to carry it out"* (Romans 7:18). While I am not advocating abandoning all efforts to change for the better, we need to understand that it is ultimately God, not us, who has the power to change us. Our obedience and surrender to Him serve to facilitate this work.

The Why of Worship

A Christian walk that centers on ourselves will ultimately affect all aspects of our relationship with God, particularly our worship. Instead of worshipping God for who He is, we will begin to worship Him for our own sake, and for what we stand to gain. When worship becomes about what we can get—whether that be peace, happiness, or identity—then we miss it. While things like peace and joy, *do* inevitably flow out of worship, they should never become the main reason we worship. When we make worship about how it can enrich us, we risk reducing it to little more than a drive-through meal. To worship God because of who He is, and because of what He has done, is reason enough. His great love is more than enough to inspire our adoration.

Keeping Sight of Eternity

Just as secular humanism encourages living for the moment,

humanistic Christianity focuses on the now, the temporal. The Enemy has propagated the lie that the world finishes at our fingertips—that our everyday concerns, the things we see, feel, and hear around us, are more real than eternity. This lie effectively keeps our focus on the things of earth, impacting our every decision and action. To break free, our eternal destiny must become more real, more tangible to us, than anything on earth—only then will we truly be able to live out our God-given mandates.

Religious Humanism vs. The Early Church

When we look to how God intends the church to be in the last days, we need to look back, rather than forward. The church of the book of Acts provides us with an ideal template for the church today. The closer we align ourselves with the principles of the early church, the more likely we are to avoid the pitfalls of religious humanism.

The early church Christians believed that:

- The highest calling of man is to engage in a deep and intimate relationship with his Creator. At the heart of this relationship are worship and surrender.
- Human beings are spirit as well as flesh and were created for communion with God. Worship, the Word, and prayer are fundamental aspects of our relationship with Him.
- The values of sacrifice and selflessness are integral to the church's mission. Individuals are part of the body of Christ and are called to work effectively together to establish the kingdom of God on earth.

Having looked at the values of the early church, we can now compare them to those of religious humanism:

Religious Humanism	The First Church
Looks to self	Looks to God
Introspective	Outward, others-focused
Beliefs based on intellect, sight, sciences.	Beliefs based upon faith and wisdom-bringing understanding to all areas of life.
Exalts human ability	Relies on God's ability
Centers on personal fulfillment	Centers upon relationship and obedience to God's will

Humanism and Universalism

Lastly, the final "destination" of Christian humanism is *universalism*. Under the premise of not judging, universalistic ideologies ultimately broaden the "narrow way" to offer more than one way to God—despite Jesus' assertion; *"I am the way and the truth and the life. No one comes to the Father except through me"* (John 14:6). Although there are many religions that acknowledge Jesus, Christianity alone *worships* Jesus—not as a prophet, or as an "enlightened one," but as *Lord*. All world religions are ultimately based on humanism, placing the onus for a person's "salvation" or "enlightenment" squarely on their own shoulders, through their own works and abilities.

Humanism is known for its inclusiveness and its ability to unite. Subsequently, it is likely to be a fundamental ideology in the end-time false religious system.

Chapter 13

❖ ❖ ❖

The Modern Grace Message

The "new kid on the block," the Modern Grace message
has become something of a worldwide sensation, from
megachurches to small congregations. As the name suggests, this
"blurred gospel" majors on God's grace. Great, right? —after all, grace
is the very essence of the Gospel. As with most false doctrines, however,
the distortions of the Modern Grace message are not found in the truth it
contains, but in what it *excludes*.

The sheer beauty of God's matchless grace is so precious, so
priceless, that it deserves to be upheld in its full, glorious splendor. Sadly
though, the Modern Grace message often cheapens biblical grace, rather
than honoring it. In his book "The Dangers of Hyper-grace," Michael L.
Brown outlines why he loves Grace:

It was John Newton, the former slave trader and the author
of "Amazing Grace," who penned the famous words, "How
precious did that grace appear the hour I first believed." I can
relate to that personally, and that's one reason I'm so jealous
for the unadulterated grace of God—grace without mixture,
grace without leaven, grace without exaggeration.[59]

In a similar vein, this chapter is in no way meant to undermine the true message of grace—a message that has utterly transformed my life—but rather to defend its purity. This is not at all an attempt either to get people back under "externally imposed religion" or legalism.[60] It is simply an honest look at the differences between the Modern Grace message and biblical grace, or, "kingdom grace."

"Dirty Words"

Strong proponents of the Modern Grace message maintain that God does not confront us with our sins, and that once we are saved we cannot experience His displeasure. The Bible paints a different picture, however. When Paul rebuked the Corinthians for eating the Lord's supper in an unworthy manner, he spoke of the real possibility of being judged and disciplined by the Lord:

> Nevertheless, when we are *judged* in this way by the Lord, we are being *disciplined* so that we will not be finally condemned with the world. (1 Corinthians 11:32, emphasis added)

Mentions of judgment and discipline do not sit easily with the Modern Grace message, and attempts are often made to explain away their presence in the New Testament. The Bible is clear, however, that God's love and correction are inseparable. Just as a loving father disciplines His children, to turn them from the wrong path, so God uses correction to guide us:

> ...Because the Lord disciplines the one he loves, and he chastens everyone he accepts as his sons. (Hebrews 12:6)

> ...Those whom I love I rebuke and discipline. So be earnest and repent. (Revelation 3:19)

Notice the order of the last verse—God affirms His love for His people, *then* brings rebuke. The two cannot be separated. God is not all love and no discipline, any more than He is all discipline and no love. Being a loving and holy God, He is compelled to bring our sins to our attention.

Does "The Comforter" Ever Make Us Uncomfortable?

In some Modern Grace circles, claims have been made that the Holy Spirit does not convict the believer of sin. After all, when God looks at us, doesn't He see only the righteousness of Christ (see 2 Corinthians 5:21)? While this is true, it is only part of the story. Although Christ's righteousness is freely available to us, we must make the decision to be clothed in it, and to flee from sin: *"Rather, clothe yourselves with the Lord Jesus Christ, and do not think about how to gratify the desires of the flesh"* (Romans 13:14). When God speaks to the churches of Revelation, He does not gloss over their conduct because of Christ's righteousness but reveals their sins, so that they might *repent.*

Some also believe that the Holy Spirit does not convict a believer of sin because He is "the Comforter." To bring sin to our attention seems to be at odds with this nature. Although the Holy Spirit is our comforter, however, we must also take into account His other names— "the Revealer" (see 1 Corinthians 2:12–16), "the Convictor," and "the Spirit of truth" (see below):

And when He has come, He will convict the world of sin, and of righteousness, and of judgment: of sin, because they do not believe in Me; of righteousness, because I go to My Father and you see Me no more; of judgment, because the ruler of this world is judged. "I still have many things to say to you, but you cannot bear them now. However, when He, the Spirit of truth, has come, He will guide you into all truth (John 16:8–13, NKJV)

Functions of The Holy Spirit

The very first task assigned to the Holy Spirit was to convict the world of sin—not to condemn, but to lead sinners to salvation. We must realize though, that He also brings conviction to believers. Notice Jesus' words in John 16:10; *"He will convict... [in regards to]...righteousness, because I go to My Father and you see Me no more."* When Jesus was no longer on the earth to guide His disciples, the Holy Spirit would fulfill this function. Just as Jesus had instructed and taught His disciples, the Holy Spirit would continue to shepherd them long after He was gone.

To guide us into all truth, the Holy Spirit must naturally bring to our attention anything unholy in our lives. Although the Modern Grace message is generally critical of feeling any negative emotions as the result of sin, the apostle Paul spoke of experiencing "godly sorrow," or remorse (not to be confused with guilt) in his rebuke to the Corinthians:

Even if I caused you sorrow by my letter, I do not regret it. Though I did regret it—I see that my letter hurt you, but only for a little while—yet now I am happy, not because you were made sorry, but because your sorrow led you to repentance. For you became sorrowful *as God intended* and so were not harmed in any way by us. Godly sorrow brings repentance that leads to salvation and leaves no regret, but worldly sorrow brings death. (2 Corinthians 7:8–10, emphasis added)

The difference between godly sorrow and guilt is that sorrow comes from grieving the Holy Spirit, while condemnation comes from the Enemy. Godly sorrow is a blessing, a God-given mechanism to bring about repentance and restore the sinner to God, while condemnation drives a wedge between God and man. Guilt is filled with regret for the past, while godly sorrow produces repentance, restoration, and hope for the future. It is possible to experience both at the same time, but as soon as we repent, guilt no longer has the legal right to accuse us.

Do I Still Have to Confess my Sins?

Some maintain that because Jesus died for our sins—past, present, and future—that it is no longer necessary for a believer to confess their sins. But is that really scriptural? Where in the Word do we find verses saying that Jesus' sacrifice on the cross negates the need to confess our sins? The closest we find, the Scripture oft quoted by grace preachers, is 1 Peter 3:18:

> For Christ also died for sins once for all, the just for the unjust, so that He might bring us to God, having been put to death in the flesh, but made alive in the spirit. (NASB)

Some have interpreted this passage to mean that Jesus died for all the sins we would ever commit, *once and for all*. Period. No confession needed ever again. But that is not what this verse is saying. The original Greek reads closer to:

> Because also Christ *once* for sin did suffer—righteous for unrighteous—that he might lead us to God, having been put to death indeed, in the flesh, and having been made alive in the spirit. (1 Peter 3:18, YLT, emphasis added)

The difference in translation is subtle but significant. The verse literally means that "Christ died *once* for sin." In other words, Jesus' *death* was a once off event, without the need to ever be repeated—rather than being "once and for all," [future] sins.

The Bible speaks of the sins we are forgiven of when we receive salvation:

> For this very reason, make every effort to add to your faith goodness; and to goodness, knowledge; and to knowledge, self-control; and to self-control, perseverance; and to perseverance, godliness; and to godliness, mutual affection;

and to mutual affection, love. For if you possess these qualities in increasing measure, they will keep you from being ineffective and unproductive in your knowledge of our Lord Jesus Christ. But whoever does not have them is nearsighted and blind, forgetting that they have been cleansed from their *past sins.* (2 Peter 1:5–9, emphasis added)

Another Scripture sometimes used to justify doing away with confession, is 1 John 1:7, PNT, emphasis added):

If we really are living in the same light in which he eternally exists, then we have true fellowship with each other, and the blood which his Son shed for us *keeps us clean* from all sin.

The premise is, that since Jesus' blood cleanses us from sin, we are perpetually clean—negating the need to confess our sins. Most translations render the Greek word used for cleanse, *katharizei,* as the present tense—"cleanses." Katharizei is more accurately translated as an ongoing action—*"the blood which his Son shed for us [continually] cleanses us from sin."*[61] As we deal with sin, confessing it, God continually sanctifies us, keeping us blameless and holy.

There are numerous biblical instances of confession—in the Old and New Testament.

Then I acknowledged my sin to you and did not cover up my iniquity. I said, "I will confess my transgressions to the Lord." And you forgave the guilt of my sin. (Psalm 32:5)

And many *who had believed* came confessing and telling their deeds. (Acts 19:18, NKJV, emphasis added)

If we confess our sins, he is faithful and just and will forgive us our sins and purify us from all unrighteousness. (1 John 1:9)

There are those who argue that confession causes us to become "sin-conscious," rather than more righteous. While I agree, that laboring under condemnation is not God's plan for us, the rationalization that the more we focus on our sins the more we will continue to sin seems counterproductive. After all, once we succeed in eliminating righteous conviction from our hearts, it actually becomes easier to continue sinning.

It has also been argued that confession is a "work." In the same way that breathing is not a "work," however, confession keeps us spiritually alive. Just as breathing draws fresh oxygen into our bodies and expels carbon dioxide, so confessing and receiving forgiveness maintains our spiritual health. As we exhale sin and breathe in God's righteousness and forgiveness, we are being transformed more into Jesus' likeness each day.

The Lawful Heart

How can a Christian know if they have committed a sin, in the first place? Does the law play any part? Citing Hebrews 8:10, some grace preachers claim that it does not—that the law has been completely done away with:

"This is the covenant I will make with the house of Israel after that time," declares the Lord. "I will put my laws in their minds and write them on their hearts. I will be their God and they will be my people." (Jeremiah 31:33)

The logic that the law has been discarded because it is now written on our hearts is flawed. God has not eliminated the law, only moved it to a different location. Although the law is no longer externally imposed on us, we now have the impulsion to do what is right *within* us, through the indwelling of the Holy Spirit. He convicts us of right and wrong *through* the law, not independently of it. Under the old covenant, the law condemned us, but under the new covenant, it alerts us to sin– that we may repent and receive God's grace. The law is not our enemy, our sinful nature is:

> What shall we say, then? Is the law sinful? Certainly not! Nevertheless, I would not have known what sin was had it not been for the law So then, the law is holy, and the commandment is holy, righteous and good. Did that which is good, then, become death to me? By no means! Nevertheless, in order that sin might be recognized as sin, it used what is good to bring about my death, so that through the commandment sin might become utterly sinful I know that good itself does not dwell in me, that is, in my sinful nature. (Romans 7:7,12–13,18)

Jesus held the law in high esteem. He made it clear that the law would not pass away until the end of the age:

> For truly I tell you, until heaven and earth disappear, not the smallest letter, not the least stroke of a pen, will by any means disappear from the Law until everything is accomplished. (Matthew 5:18)

As new covenant believers, we are not under the law, nor above it. Despite our inability to keep all of the Ten Commandments, Jesus has graciously fulfilled the requirements of the law for us (see Matthew 5:17). All that is left for us to do is to take hold of His righteousness, through repentance.

For He Himself is our peace, who has made both one, and

has broken down the middle wall of separation, having abolished in His flesh the enmity, that is, the law of commandments contained in ordinances, so as to create in Himself one new man from the two, thus making peace. (Ephesians 2:14–15, NKJV)

Once Saved Always Saved?

The Modern Grace message is built upon the doctrine of "eternal security" or, "once saved, always saved." This belief is built upon the assumption that it is impossible to lose one's salvation, and that once a believer has been sealed by the Holy Spirit (see Ephesians 1:13, 4:30), their eternal destiny is fixed. There are many Scriptures to the contrary, however—too many to include. My hope is that the few verses included in this chapter will serve as a springboard for you to conduct your own personal study into the topic.

The key to refuting the doctrine of eternal security is having an understanding of the Book of Life. Before the foundation of the world, the names of those who would inherit eternal life were written in this book (see Revelation 13:8, 17:8). Many believe that once an individual's name is written in there, it cannot be removed. Scripture shows, however, that it is possible for a person to have their name blotted out of the book:

So Moses went back to the Lord and said, "Oh, what a great sin these people have committed! They have made themselves gods of gold. But now, please forgive their sin— but if not, then blot me out of the book you have written. (Exodus 32:31–32)

May they be blotted out of the book of life and not be listed with the righteous. (Psalm 69:28)

The one who is victorious will, like them, be dressed in white. I will never blot out the name of that person from

99

the book of life, but will acknowledge that name before my Father and his angels. (Revelation 3:5)

The apostle Paul's repeated exhortations guard our eternal salvation are also completely at odds with the doctrine of eternal security.

Watch your life and doctrine closely. Persevere in them, because if you do, you will save both yourself and your hearers. (1 Timothy 4:16)

But you, man of God, flee from all this, and pursue righteousness, godliness, faith, love, endurance and gentleness. Fight the good fight of the faith. Take hold of the eternal life to which you were called when you made your good confession in the presence of many witnesses. (1 Timothy 6:11-12)

Paul mentions that it is possible to *"fall away from the faith"* (see 1 Tim 4:1) and be *"shipwrecked in the faith"* (1 Tim 1:19). Once we have made the confession of faith, we are not the holders of an eternal "get out of jail free" pass, free to live as we like. We are instructed to *"hold fast to our confession"* (see Hebrews 10:23) and to *"work out"* our salvation:

Therefore, my dear friends, as you have always obeyed— not only in my presence, but now much more in my absence—continue to work out your salvation with fear and trembling... (Philippians 2:12)

The phrase "work out" comes from the Greek word *katergazomai*; literally meaning "work down to the end-point."[62] Salvation is the end point, and the journey starts when we accept Christ. Please understand that this does not mean, in any way, that our salvation is works-based.

Notice that the verse says, *"work out your salvation,"* not *"work [for] your salvation."* Salvation is something to be guarded and protected.

While it is true, we are adopted as God's children by grace alone, when we accept Christ as the Lord of our lives, we have the obligation to live for Him. This means that we are committed to doing His will and walking in obedience. James makes it clear that while man is not justified by works alone, his faith is strengthened and made complete through his actions:

> But someone will say, "You have faith; I have deeds." Show me your faith without deeds, and I will show you my faith by my deeds. You foolish person, do you want evidence that faith without deeds is useless? Was not our father Abraham considered righteous for what he did when he offered his son Isaac on the altar? You see that his faith and his actions were working together, and his faith was made complete by what he did. And the scripture was fulfilled that says, "Abraham believed God, and it was credited to him as righteousness," and he was called God's friend. You see that a person is considered righteous by what they do and not by faith alone. (James 2:18, 20:24)

If we continue to live in ungodliness, we demonstrate that we are not abiding in Christ and never had a deep relationship with him—*"No one who lives in him keeps on sinning. No one who continues to sin has either seen him or known him"* (1 John 3:6). Without sanctification, it is possible to fall short of the grace of God:

> Make every effort to live in peace with everyone and to be holy; without holiness no one will see the Lord. See to it that no one falls short of the grace of God and that no bitter root grows up to cause trouble and defile many. (Hebrews 12:14–15)

The Point of No Return

If we choose to pursue ungodliness, it is possible to reach a point when the Holy Spirit ceases to strive with us. This happened to King Saul—*"Now the Spirit of the Lord had departed from Saul, and an evil spirit from the Lord tormented him"* (1 Samuel 16:14). To cause the Holy Spirit to depart from us is to endanger our own souls—He is our seal, a *"deposit guaranteeing our inheritance until the redemption of those who are God's possession"* (Ephesians 1:14).

God is infinitely merciful, and allows every opportunity for an individual to repent and turn from sin. After falling into adultery with Bathsheba, David begged God—*"Do not cast me from your presence or take your Holy Spirit from me"* (Psalm 51:11). David understood that it was possible for the Holy Spirit to be taken from him, and was overcome with grief at the prospect (perhaps it was after witnessing Saul's demise that he became aware of this very real possibility). God honored David's request, and he became known as a "man after God's own heart."

Two men fell in sin, with totally different outcomes. Saul's moral failure estranged him from God, while David's brought him closer. What made all the difference was how each man chose to respond to sin. David ultimately confronted his sin. Saul did not. David ran to God, Saul ran away. David was restored, but Saul was destroyed by his sin. If we follow David's model each time we fall—if we confront our sins, taking them to God, and are restored, we will continue to dwell in and foster His presence in our lives.

The Giver of the Gift

While grace is the greatest gift we could receive, it is just that—a gift. How much it must grieve the Father's heart when we focus more on His gift of grace than our relationship with Him, the Giver! When we begin to see grace, not just as a gift, but as a beautiful expression of God's character, it will draw us deeper into our relationship with Him.

Chapter 14

❖ ❖ ❖

The "Mystic" Gospel

On our travels, we have had the great joy of witnessing firsthand the present outpouring of the Holy Spirit in churches across the globe. We have seen amazing miracles and healings, as God lavishes His presence on His people. These truly are the days spoken of by the prophet Joel, when God's Spirit will be poured out upon all flesh (see Joel 2:28–29).

Sadly though (and as is the case with all great moves of God), the Enemy is trying his best to contaminate what God is doing with false teaching and unscriptural practices. Before I go any further, let me state emphatically that there *are* true, genuine outpourings of the Spirit—I urge you not to throw out the proverbial baby with the bathwater. It is possible for us to exercise discernment *and* be open to the Spirit's leading. Just as the existence of a counterfeit painting does not devalue the original, the Enemy's forgeries should inspire us to cherish the true manifestations of the Spirit all the more.

In this chapter, we will be looking at a third blurred gospel—the new age "Mystic" gospel.

If it Looks Like, Sounds Like...

To understand the presence of the new age in the church, we must first be aware that the "new" age is anything but new—it hails from ancient Babylon, where Nimrod sought to usher in a "new era" of religion by creating a synthesis of many pagan practices.

In modern times, the new age has crept into the church so subtly that it is often hard to detect. If in doubt, a good rule to apply is—if it "looks like, sounds like, and feels like," then there is a good chance it is. There are features unique to the "Mystic" gospel that can also help you identify it:

1) A Fixation on the Experiential

The Mystic gospel often encourages a mania for new supernatural experiences and manifestations. While legitimate encounters with God *are* a biblical and vital part of our Christian walks, when we begin to pursue supernatural experiences purely for the "kick" they give, we risk giving legal entry to the Enemy's deception.

2) Mystic Spirituality and Elements of Paganism

When you hear of believers looking to "ancient" wisdom for guidance in their Christian walk, there is a pretty good chance they have come across "Christian" mysticism. Mysticism in a worship service may feature instruments traditionally associated with pagan rituals (such as trance-inducing instruments or instruments used to call up spirits). Although instruments are not inherently good or bad in themselves, the rule of "sounds like" must be applied. The Spirit of God will help you discern if there is a spirit other than His Holy Spirit in operation.

3) An Obsession with Angelic Encounters

Mysticism and the new age also majors on angels and angelic encounters. Although angelic visitations are by no means unscriptural, the Word warns us about being fixated with angels; *"Let no one cheat you of your reward, taking delight in false humility and worship of angels "* (Colossians 2:18, NKJV). We are also warned of receiving any "revelation," that contradicts the Word; *"But even if we, or an angel from heaven, preach any other gospel to you than what we have preached to you, let him be accursed,"* (Galatians 1:8, NKJV).

4) The Use of New Age Techniques such as Meditation

In some mystic-style meetings, it is not uncommon for new age practices to be used. Believers are commonly urged to throw all caution and reason to the wind and are berated for their "lack of faith" if they seem hesitant (on some occasions I have seen ministers condemn those reluctant to participate as being "religious"). This type of "faith" is actually a psychological state called "the willing suspension of disbelief"—the same state we adopt to enjoy watching a movie we know to be untrue. The suspension of disbelief is needed to undertake another new age practice—"emptying" or "freeing" the mind. When an individual enters this state, totally letting down their spiritual guard, they are left vulnerable to counterfeit experiences. It should be noted that, while overanalyzing *can* hinder us from receiving the Spirit, there are no scriptural instances of the Holy Spirit overriding a person's will.

At a Christian meeting I attended several years ago, everyone in the room was instructed to lie flat on their back with their eyes closed. In a low, sing-song voice, the visiting speaker encouraged people to clear all distractions from their minds and to be open to the supernatural experiences they were about to have. As I listened, I felt uncomfortable without knowing why. The tone of voice, the words, the concept—it all sounded familiar. Then it dawned on me. I had heard almost an identical spiel in class, as a young university student. In a lesson typical of the strongly new age arts course I was studying, the class had undertaken a "guided meditation." The "sanctified" version at the meeting followed a near-identical format.

Without going into detail, most of the visions people shared after the guided meditation were quite bizarre. Sadly though, they all had one thing in common—a huge dose of novelty, revealing nothing of the greatness of God.

5) Unchecked Chaos

Lastly, where there is a new age influence, chaos often runs riot. The lack of order is often framed as "freedom in the Spirit," and justified with Scriptures such as 2 Corinthians 3:17; *"Now the Lord is the Spirit, and where the Spirit of the Lord is, there is freedom."* The Word also states, however, that *"the spirits of prophets are subject to the control of prophets. For God is not a God of disorder but of peace—as in all the congregations of the Lord's people"* (1 Corinthians 14:32–33).

These two Scriptures do not cancel each other out; but rather, they balance one another. To be fair, those who argue that structure in the church quenches the Spirit usually do so out of a genuine dissatisfaction. Many have become tired of the status quo, of a system restricted by programs and man's agendas. Unfortunately, though, this can often lead to another extreme—of total disorder. When meetings operate this way, it is not unusual for "spiritual manifestations" to erupt noisily during the preaching, even interrupting the flow of God's Word.

Discerning the Spirits

Here are some basic questions you can use to gauge any spiritual manifestations you feel a check in your spirit about:

1.) Who does the manifestation draw attention to?

If the manifestation does little else other than draw attention to an individual, particularly in a way that is indulgent and distracting, then spiritual deception may be in operation. A true manifestation of the Spirit will point to God, revealing His glory. The Holy Spirit will always inspire us to awestruck reverence and worship—He loves to bring honor to the Father and Son.

One of the most touching encounters with God I have ever come across happened to four precious girls at a school camp. As they lay on their dormitory beds one night, trying to fall asleep, the girls had a corporate vision of Jesus. When they relayed the vision to me the next day, the girls spoke excitedly of how tall and mighty Jesus looked, and of how He lovingly scooped them up in His arms. As He talked with them, they were overwhelmed by His beauty. The girls' eyes sparkled as they spoke and I could see God's presence shining on their faces. The overwhelming message they received from the vision was how much Jesus loved them. The fact that He was the very center of their experience left me with no doubt that the encounter was genuine.

2.) Do the manifestations contradict the Word?

When experiences are feelings-based over Word-based, error abounds. Godly supernatural experiences should not only flow out of our communion with the Spirit but be firmly grounded in the Word. When manifestations are not held up to the standard of Scripture, the waters can quickly become muddied. There are those, for example, who claim to have communicated with female angels. There are also spiritual practices that, although scriptural, must be properly understood. Meditation is referred to over thirty times in the Word. Most references are found in the Psalms, suggesting that meditation played an integral part in the writers' personal walks with the Lord: *"I call to remembrance my song in the night; I meditate within my heart, and my spirit makes diligent search"* (Psalm 77:6, NKJV).

To know the biblical definition of meditation, we must understand that it differs from the world's definition. The aim of new age meditation is to clear or "empty" the mind of all distractions and achieve spiritual awakening (or, "enlightenment"). True biblical meditation, on the other hand, is to focus on and fill our minds with the things of God, until He saturates our whole hearts, minds, souls, and spirits. The psalmists meditated on topics such as:

- God's laws and precepts (Psalm 1:2, 119:15,23,48,78)
- God's promises (Psalm 119:148)
- God's ways (Psalm 119:15)
- God's mighty deeds (Psalm 77:12, 145:5)
- The work of God's hands (Psalm 143:5)

We can use these areas as inspiration for our own times of meditation. *Hagah*, the Hebrew word for meditation, can also be translated as: "to make a sound," "mutter," "ponder," or "utter." *Hagah* is to ruminate on the Word until it literally bubbles up from our innermost being. As we dwell on God, allowing our hearts and minds to "marinate" in His Word, we will see godly transformation pervade every area of our lives.

3.)   **What are the Fruits?**

Another factor to take into consideration when weighing a supernatural experience is the resulting fruit. Does the experience cause an individual to grow in their walk with God? Does it result in a greater thirst for holiness, or does the person continue to live as before? Lastly, does the experience inspire someone to a greater reverence for God, or does it cause them to make light of the things of God? This calls for careful discernment—it is also possible for a believer to experience a genuine manifestation of the Holy Spirit, but to mishandle it, through lack of character.

God is gracious, and will even pour out His Spirit even on those who are not walking wholeheartedly in His ways (for a *time*). He is patient, desiring that we allow Him to work in us and change us. Ultimately though, a believer who truly walks in the anointing will bring forth the fruits of the Spirit; *"love, joy, peace, patience, kindness, goodness, faithfulness, gentleness and self-control"* (Galatians 5:22–23).

Safe Guarding Against the New Age

Knowing how to identify false spiritual manifestations is one way to safeguard your spirit. Secondly, and most importantly, we must maintain an intimate walk with God. The more know God's character, the less likely we will be to accept anything other than His Spirit.

Imagine for a moment you are approached by someone you have never met before, who accuses a close family member of doing something completely uncharacteristic. What would you do? Would you be outraged? Would you rush to your relative's defense? In the same way, if we truly *know* God, we will be quick to identify anything that is not of Him. Only by knowing Him intimately can we recognize His voice and accurately discern the works of His hands:

> My sheep listen to my voice; I know them, and they follow me. I give them eternal life, and they shall never perish; no one will snatch them out of my hand. (John 10:27–28)

Chapter 15

The Gospel of More

The rise and fall of the Prosperity gospel can be directly correlated to the world's economy. In times of great economic prosperity, this blurred gospel has also flourished—during the economic boom of the eighties, for example. Since the GFC in 2008, however, it seems that the Prosperity gospel's popularity has waned somewhat, with believers becoming more cynical towards its message. It actually saddens my heart to see this, because the Prosperity gospel (along with the all the other blurred gospels), actually contains much truth. It is unfortunate that many of these truths have become distorted beyond recognition. In this chapter, we will be separating these distortions from the truths that many are now questioning and discarding.

Prosperity Gospel Fundamentals

The Prosperity gospel revolves around two key beliefs, namely that;

1) A believer's life should predominately be marked by victory, success and financial prosperity, and,

2) A believer's level of success (particularly in finances), is ultimately tied to their level of faith.

John 10:10 is often quoted in support of these beliefs; *"The thief comes only to steal and kill and destroy; I have come that they may have life, and have it to the full."* But what is biblical prosperity, really? Is the "full" or "abundant" life Jesus spoke of a reference to material prosperity, or is it something else?

The Word tells us that a truly abundant life is, first and foremost, one that has been made complete in the riches of salvation:

> I pray that the eyes of your heart may be enlightened in order that you may know the hope to which he has called you, the riches of his glorious inheritance in his holy people. (Ephesians 1:18)

An abundant life is one that has been ransomed from the power of sin and death, and redeemed in Jesus Christ! True prosperity begins in our souls. It is a prosperity that causes us to grow in character and in faith each day—in obedience to God's will.

When Life Seems Not-So-Abundant

One area of Christian life that has been glossed over, and at times almost stigmatized by the Prosperity gospel, is hardship. In other words, if a believer walks in abundant faith, they should consequently walk in perpetual victory. The apostle Paul's experiences (as well as many heroes of the Faith) paint a different picture:

> Whatever anyone else dares to boast about—I am speaking as a fool—I also dare to boast about. Are they Hebrews? So am I. Are they Israelites? So am I. Are they Abraham's descendants? So am I. Are they servants of Christ? (I am out of my mind to talk like this.) I am more. I have worked much harder, been in prison more frequently, been flogged more severely, and been exposed to death again and again. Five times I received from the Jews the forty lashes minus one. Three times I was beaten with rods, once I was pelted with

stones, three times I was shipwrecked, I spent a night and a day in the open sea, I have been constantly on the move. I have been in danger from rivers, in danger from bandits, in danger from my fellow Jews, in danger from Gentiles; in danger in the city, in danger in the country, in danger at sea; and in danger from false believers. I have labored and toiled and have often gone without sleep; I have known hunger and thirst and have often gone without food; I have been cold and naked. Besides everything else, I face daily the pressure of my concern for all the churches. *Who is weak, and I do not feel weak? Who is led into sin, and I do not inwardly burn? If I must boast, I will boast of the things that show my weakness.* (2 Corinthians 11:21–30, emphasis added)

Had Paul been alive today, he would not have been a poster boy for the Prosperity gospel. His long list of struggles, including persecution and physical lack, present a dilemma for proponents of the Prosperity gospel.

Biblical Victory

At this point you may well be wondering, "am I then to accept suffering or hardship as my lot—the Bible *does* say I have the victory, doesn't it?" While we certainly do, as always, the truth here lies somewhere between two extremes. The Prosperity gospel paints victory as a mindset, leading to extreme success. The Bible, on the other hand, paints victory as the heart-attitude of an overcomer. Biblical victory does not require external circumstances to change for the believer to experience freedom:

I know what it is to be in need, and I know what it is to have plenty. I have learned the secret of being content in any and every situation, whether well fed or hungry, whether living in plenty or in want. I can do all this through him who gives me strength. (Philippians 4:12–13)

Faith Confessions and God's Will

The Prosperity gospel encourages believers to exercise their faith, particularly by confessing the Word. This *is* a mighty revelation—faith and confession are powerful together. The Word contains the resurrection power of Jesus Christ. It unleashes His power into every area of our lives and beings, bringing light to the darkness and overcoming every stronghold:

> For the word of God is alive and active. Sharper than any double-edged sword, it penetrates even to dividing soul and spirit, joints and marrow; it judges the thoughts and attitudes of the heart. (Hebrews 4:12)

The Word is so powerful because it is *"God-breathed!"* (See 2 Tim 3:16.) Let's ponder that for a moment. When God created the world, He sent forth The Word, Jesus Christ, who made creation manifest by the power of the Holy Spirit (see Genesis 1:1–2). We are created in God's image. Because of this, the words we speak also carry power—for life or death (see Proverbs 18:21).

Because God's Word always lines up with His will, when we speak the Word, we speak the very plans and purposes of God. The Prosperity gospel encourages confession as a mechanism to bring forth our own success. Biblical confession, on the other hand, brings us into agreement with God's will, causing us to speak His promises into being. Faith confessions are not meant to be "incantations;" used for getting what we want, but are to be expressions of our trust in God, tied to our obedience:

> This is the confidence we have in approaching God; that if we ask anything *according to his will*, he hears us. And if we

know that he hears us—whatever we ask—we know that we have what we asked of him. (1 John 5:14, emphasis added)

Dear friends, if our hearts do not condemn us, we have confidence before God and receive from him anything we ask, because we keep his commands and do what pleases him. (1 John 3:21–22)

Is it Easy to be in God's Will?

A few years back, Alejandro and I felt led by God to make a major life decision and step into a new area. It was not easy, and we faced many challenges. Noticing our struggles, a well-meaning friend of ours enquired, "Are you sure you are in the will of God?" "Why is that?" we asked. He shrugged. "Well, if we're in the will of God, it isn't that hard, is it? I mean, shouldn't everything just fall into place?"

Our friend's observation reflects the popular belief that, if we are in God's will, life will go smoothly. In many instances, though, the very opposite is true—often it is right in the center of God's will that we must push the hardest through trials and opposition.

Even if we are making faith confessions in accordance with God's will, we will still experience hardship from time to time. As Jesus promised us, *"in this world, you will have trouble"* (John 16:33). As counter intuitive as it may seem, we will sometimes experience times of difficulty—even as part of God's will.

Dear friends, do not be surprised at the fiery ordeal that has come on you to test you, as though something strange were happening to you... However, if you suffer as a Christian, do not be ashamed, but praise God that you bear that name... So then, those who suffer *according to God's will* should commit themselves to their faithful Creator and continue to do good. (1 Peter 4:12,16,19, emphasis added)

True Giving

Biblical giving has two primary purposes: firstly, it is an act of worship, honoring God as our Provider and as the Lord of our lives; *"Honor the Lord with your wealth, with the firstfruits of all your crops,"* (Proverbs 3:9). Secondly, our giving is to be used for God's purposes, for the expansion of His kingdom. The Prosperity gospel often emphasizes giving to God and receiving back, (i.e. the more I give, the more I will receive) rather than giving to God because it glorifies Him.

The Word cautions us against setting our thoughts and affections on money—something that is all too easy to do:

> No one can serve two masters. Either you will hate the one and love the other, or you will be devoted to the one and despise the other. You cannot serve both God and money. (Matthew 6:24)

Our best line of defense against the "Gospel of More" is to place our trust squarely in God—not in the material. In this way, our tithing and giving is a reflection of that trust.

Chapter 16

❖ ❖ ❖

Discerning Godly Ministry

In the last days, even the elect will be deceived (see Matthew 24:24). Armed with this knowledge, we must carefully sift what teaching we allow into our lives and carefully choose the ministries we allow to minister us. You can use the following questions as a guideline:

Questions to Ask

↪ Is there an overemphasis on money and financial blessings? What are the primary reasons for giving—to honor God or gain increase?

↪ Does the ministry/minister operate in genuine humility? Is the ministry built on the minister's charisma and personality, or is it focused on bringing glory to God?

↪ Does the preaching/teaching line up with the Word? Are there any conspicuous absences or "gaps" in the preaching of the Word? Is any extra-biblical revelation taught, either explicitly or implied?

↪ Is there an overemphasis on supernatural manifestations and spiritual experiences?

↪ Are believers encouraged to override any legitimate concerns they may have, throwing all caution to the wind?

↪ Lastly, does the ministry/minister operate in love?

This last question is perhaps the most important. One of the traits of Jesus' earthly ministry was love—it remains the hallmark of a truly godly ministry. Love demonstrates that we know God and that He ministers through us:

> Dear friends, let us love one another, for love comes from God. Everyone who loves has been born of God and knows God. Whoever does not love does not know God, because God is love. (1 John 4:7–8)

Love does not mean that a ministry is "soft" and ineffective. During His earthly ministry, for example, Jesus often put his finger on an area holding a person captive. But the truth of His words was always tempered by love—in fact, it was love that *drove* Jesus to address issues in people's lives.

Discernment vs. Criticism

May love be the hallmark of how we speak to, and of, those who have strayed from the Word. Most are sincere people, devoted to the things of God. These questions are not intended to be used to criticize ministries, individuals, or the church, but rather, to help you guard your heart. There is no ministry on earth that is perfect—the questions are not intended to be used as a "test" that a ministry or church must pass. If you feel that your church or the ministry you are under is operating in significant error, I would urge you to prayerfully bring this before God. Be rooted where He has called you to be, for the season He has called you to be there. Continue to fellowship faithfully, *"not giving up meeting together, as some are in the habit of doing, but encouraging one another—and all the more as [we] see the Day approaching"* (Hebrews 10:25)

PART FOUR:

Becoming Revelation Ready

❖ ❖ ❖

Chapter 17

The Alarm Goes off

A lejandro and I sat in the car, stupefied. For several minutes, all we could do was stare at the windshield. Finally, Alejandro broke the silence. "It's all so much more...I don't know, *real* now," he said softly. "It's actually happening. I mean, we're already *in it*." I paused for a long time before responding. *"We may not have as much time as we thought."*

Around three years ago, Alejandro and I experienced something of a spiritual awakening. We were active in the church, in full-time ministry, and deeply committed to the Lord. Unknown to us, however, we were lacking in a key area—we were totally unaware of the spiritual *time*.

Has your alarm ever failed to go off, specifically when you had to wake up early for a meeting or to catch a flight? Remember the awful shock you got after awakening leisurely, naturally, then registering the actual time? That's the very same feeling we had while sitting in a conference about the last days, several years ago. God used two anointed prophets to sound the alarm loud and clear in our spirits. As we listened to them, the Holy Spirit branded their words into our hearts. Hours felt like minutes—we could have sat listening all night. The urgency the prophets spoke with was so profound, that it took weeks after our conversation in the car for us to fully "digest" all we had heard, and fully grasp what God was saying to us. Our perception of the last days as some far-off event on the horizon shifted drastically—our "clocks" jumped forward, from 11:45 p.m. to 11:59 p.m. This new understanding of the times injected a renewed urgency, drive, and purposefulness into our lives.

Dear friend, it is not enough for us to simply observe the events unfolding today, speculating on what is going wrong with the world. We need to be proactive. Armed with the knowledge of how we are to live and how we can guard our hearts, we must move forward– understanding that we are on the offensive, not the defensive. The questions in this section are designed to help you determine your level of readiness for the days to come. The "checklist" is not intended to show up your failures, but rather, to guide you into a greater level of preparation.

❖ ❖ ❖

Chapter 18

Check #1:
Am I Aware of the Times?

All of our days, from the moment we get up, to the moment we fall asleep each night, are driven by *time*. Our actions and daily schedules revolve around *time*. In the same way, knowing the "spiritual time" can give our lives a greater sense of purpose.

All actions flow out of our convictions. Accordingly, if we believe without a doubt that we are living in the last days, our actions will reflect this conviction. We are to live with a sense of urgency—not a frantic, fear-based urgency, but an urgency that comes from having a fierce sense of purpose, in light of eternity.

Aware, yet Unafraid

Jesus taught us in Mark 13:7 that it is possible to live with a sense of urgency, with our eyes wide open to the events around us, and yet be unafraid; *"When you hear of wars and rumors of wars, do not be alarmed. Such things must happen, but the end is still to come."* The phrase, *"do not be alarmed!"* is a mandate for all believers.

In the last days, those who have true peace will stand out like lighthouses in an increasingly fearful world. As the world splinters into increasingly broken fragments, many will turn to believers, seeking an explanation for what they see unfolding. We need to not only be able to interpret the times, but to offer peace and assurance.

A Choice Weapon

As Satan prepares for his final skirmish with humanity, he will try more than ever to paralyze and render God's children ineffective through fear. Fear operates like a parasite. It sucks the faith out of a believer, weakening their soul. It causes us to doubt God's character, whispering lies such as; "will He *really* protect you?" Over time, these lies lead us to take our focus off God's supernatural power and limit us to see only in the natural.

Ironically, when we accept that living in these times involves an element of danger, we can be at peace, knowing that we are not our own protectors. God alone knows if and when we may face dangerous circumstances. In our human efforts, there is no way we can totally insulate ourselves from what is to come, and there is no place on earth that will not feel the shaking. God never removes the element of trust from our walk with Him. He will guide us through each situation we face, as we lean on Him. Our best preparation is to fill ourselves with His promises, rather than feed our souls with fear.

Comfort vs. Faith

I will be the first to admit that being faith-filled, not "fear-full" can be a challenge. When God called Alejandro and me to move to the United States, I felt somewhat apprehensive at the prospect. I would be moving away from my family and away from the country I had known all my life. For years before receiving the word, Alejandro and I would sit in our living room each night, watching the American news on cable TV, and marveling at the social and political upheaval we saw. I felt... comfortable, though. That was *over there*. And then God called us to move *over there*.

God graciously filled me with peace during the long months of sorting out visas and moving arrangements. Once I arrived in the US, however, I began to battle fear again. The first week after we arrived, a tornado made landfall just a mile away from us, shredding an entire neighborhood. I had never been close to a tornado in my life, so this was quite a new experience! When I received an "imminent tornado threat" alert on my cell phone, I literally had no idea what to do.

Since then, I have had to face the fear of tornados on several occasions—the time in Oklahoma, for example, when a severe storm formed behind us and seemed to follow us along the highway! Needless to say, I am now well-versed in tornado safety! On our travels overseas, we have also encountered many precarious situations that we had no control over. Strangely though, these circumstances have turned out to be precious, drawing us closer to God and growing our faith in Him.

Moving Past Fear

So how then should we proceed, with all that is taking place around us?

Firstly, we must abide in God. To abide means to live like He is our oxygen—as though we truly, *"live, breathe, move and have our being in Him"* (Acts 17:28). To abide means to make God the center of all we do, rather than some sort of spiritual add-on to our lives.

Today we live in the digital age when there is an app for everything. Want to get fit? No problems, there's an app for that! Want to get parenting tips, track your spending, store your documents, get ideas for home décor, connect with a business network or edit your pictures? There's an app for that!

Once I overheard a teacher colleague of mine lamenting the fact that his students didn't seem to want to learn. "Don't worry, there's an app for that!" my boss remarked, grinning. The point is, we must not risk relegating our relationship with God to the level of some sort of spiritual app. Have a physical need? There's a prayer app for that. Feel like social interaction? There's a small group app for that.

When we make God the center of all we do, on the other hand, *who* we are becomes totally wrapped up in Him. When we abide in Him, we are *hidden* in Him. No matter what we face, we can face it enveloped in His person—the One who does not change with the times; the One who is not relative but absolute. He is the same yesterday, today and forever. As the world becomes a darker place, He never changes. We can take great comfort in this fact.

Secondly, we must stay finely attuned to God's voice, with listening ears and listening hearts. A trust-building exercise, called "minefield," Illustrates the importance of listening to God. It is an activity for two people, one of whom is blindfolded. The person who is not blindfolded must verbally guide their partner through a maze of obstacles, such as chairs strewn around the room. The aim is to guide your partner successfully from one end of the room to another, without touching a "minefield." In the same way, taking the time to hear clearly from God can be the difference between stepping on secure footing or stepping on a "spiritual minefield."

To be led by God's is to come under His covering. A few years ago, a couple approached us after a church service and shared their remarkable story. One day, they had suddenly felt led to pack up their valuables and leave their house. God gave them the sense that an impending disaster was about to strike. Just a few days later, the deadliest bushfire in Australian history scorched through 1737 square miles of Victorian land. The disaster that became known as the Black Saturday bushfires left unprecedented destruction in its wake. Incredibly, the very same God who instructed Joseph to evacuate the infant Messiah's family to Egypt, God who instructed Noah to build an ark, and who walked in the fiery furnace with the three Babylonian exiles, had led this couple to safety. God protected them as they sought Him, and He can do the same for you.

If the Son of God needed to hear His father's voice for daily guidance, then how much more do we? I imagine Jesus praying each morning, receiving a "briefing" from His General—information on the enemy's location perhaps, places to avoid, and Jesus' destination and assignments for the day.

Just as Jesus was "invincible" for the plans and purposes of God (even as He hung on the cross), nothing can destroy us when we are fully committed to God's will. No matter what happens or what hardships you may experience, you can face tomorrow in the security that *"He who began a good work in you will carry it on to completion"* (Philippians 1:6).

We cannot live a life of "what-if's," simply because of the times we are living in—*"what if* I face persecution, *what if* the economy collapses, what if, what if, *what if....?"* The list is endless. There is only one way, and it is forward. The more we advance, the further fear will fall by the wayside.

Chapter 19

———— ❖ ❖ ❖ ————

Check #2:
Am I Exercising Discernment?

In the last days, it is vital that we pray earnestly for discernment. Without it, we are restricted to operating only on what we see in the natural:

> The person without the Spirit does not accept the things that come from the Spirit of God but considers them foolishness, and cannot understand them because they are discerned only through the Spirit. (1 Corinthians 2:14)

Discernment gives us the spiritual insight to respond to situations and people with wisdom, rather than out of our limited understanding. It helps us understand the hidden dimensions of a problem we face. Say, for example, you had a business that was failing. There could be a range of possibilities why;

a) The business' finances could have been managed better; you need to ask God for new strategies;

b) God could be closing the door for your business because He is leading you in another direction;

c) A curse of poverty needs to be broken off the business for it to succeed;

Activating your God-given discernment is essential for you to be able to accurately assess the situation and implement an appropriate strategy.

As well as the discernment to make good decisions, the Bible speaks of two other types: the ability to distinguish, or judge, what is corrupt from what is pure; and the discerning of spirits. In a "fifty shades of morality" society, our discernment of good and evil needs to stay razor sharp. As mature believers, we must be alert, ready to activate this tool at any given moment:

> But solid food is for those who are of full age, that is, those who by reason of use have their senses exercised to discern both good and evil. (Hebrews 5:14, NKJV)

The discerning of spirits enables us to test what types of spirits are in operation in a given situation.

> Dear friends, do not believe every spirit, but test the spirits to see whether they are from God, because many false prophets have gone out into the world. (1 John 4:1)

This type of discernment is crucial, particularly as supernatural manifestations increase upon the earth (both good and bad), and as the antichrist spirit attempts to pervade all spheres of society:

> For false messiahs and false prophets will appear and perform signs and wonders... (Mark 13:22)

How do I get discernment?

Discernment is received through prayer and by reading the Word, but is *activated* by the Holy Spirit. Just as the Holy Spirit causes the Word to come alive in our hearts as supernatural revelation, we cannot move in discernment without the Spirit's unction. We need to be willing to let go of our own natural thinking to receive true discernment.

About two years ago, Alejandro and I ministered in a church in South Western Australia. During the altar call, I had the opportunity to pray for a young lady. My heart went out to her; as we prayed, God showed me that she had gone through many hurtful experiences and was in deep emotional pain. I asked God to reveal His message to her and He gave me a word of knowledge. In my heart, I longed to comfort her, but the Spirit was saying something very different. Like a doctor, taking old dressings off a wound, He went straight to the root of the issues she had been dealing with. He revealed the anger and bitterness she had been carrying inside and her need to forgive.

As I was delivering the word, the woman doubled over as though she had been punched in the stomach and tears filled her eyes. "Oh no!" I thought, "what have I done? I must have missed it—she needs love and consolation, not a confrontation!"

The Holy Spirit gently broke these thoughts, bringing me back on course. "Rebekah, she is not ready," He said. "It grieves me, but no matter what is said to her tonight, she is not ready or willing to be free." "Why Lord?" I asked. "Because she is held captive by a spirit of self-pity," He said. "She has become comfortable living with it and refuses to let go—it has become like an emotional crutch in her life."

I continued to pray with the woman for a little longer, speaking to her of the steps she could take when ready to receive her freedom. All of a sudden, her whole demeanor changed. Her face snapped from wounded to enraged, confirming what the Spirit had shown me. It saddens me to know that she left the church that night, still bound—and it is my prayer that someday she will remember the word given to her and will be set free.

I learned a very important lesson from this experience—our own minds and will can hinder us from receiving discernment. To be open to receive true discernment, we must operate, not only in love but in obedience, willing to lay down our own perceptions and thoughts. Gaining discernment is a matter of *asking, listening* and *receiving*. When I prayed for the young woman, I *asked* God for revelation, I *listened* to His response, then I *received* it in obedience.

Sometimes we do not receive discernment simply because we do not ask, (see James 4:2). The Word assures us that if we ask for divine wisdom, we will receive it: *"If anyone lacks wisdom, let him ask of God, who gives to all liberally and without reproach, and it will be given to him"* (James 1:5, NKJV).

Lastly, to gain discernment, we must earnestly desire it, pursuing it until we lay hold of it:

For if you cry for discernment, lift your voice for understanding; if you seek her as silver and search for her as for hidden treasures; then you will discern the fear of the LORD and discover the knowledge of God. (Proverbs 2:3–5, NASB)

❖ ❖ ❖

Chapter 20

Check #3:
Am I Walking in Righteousness?

Righteousness is powerful. Jesus was only able to defeat the Enemy on the cross because of His utter righteousness. We are told that the prayers of a righteous man are effective (see James 5:16). Righteousness is so effective because it carries *authority*. For this reason, the Enemy is doing all he can today to get believers to hand over their God-given authority. The number one ways he does this is through compromise.

To compromise is to form an ungodly alliance with the world, accepting its standards as our own. Often compromise comes under the guise of becoming more "tolerant" and "accepting." Packaged in shiny political correctness, it seems like the "right thing" to do. By assuaging the guilt of the human conscience, compromise offers a false sense of self-righteousness.

Around 60 years ago, the changes we are seeing in society and the legislations being passed would have been unimaginable. We are seeing the world embrace a "morality" that calls *"evil good and good evil"* (Isaiah 5:20). It is in this context that we must make the decision to hold firmly to what is right, with the tenacity of a drowning man clinging to a rock.

Righteousness and Relationship

True righteousness can only well up out of an intimate relationship with God—we desire to do what is right out of our love for Him. When we know and love God intimately, we will:

a) Become acutely aware of when we have grieved the Holy Spirit.
b) Have the security that we can bring our "messes" to Him, even the "ugliest" ones.
c) Understand that we cannot live righteously by our own efforts and striving.

King David recognized that God alone could create a pure heart within him. He did not trust in his own strength to do right. Interestingly, David did not pray "Lord, I am willing to do what is right," instead, he asked God to *give* him a willing spirit, that he might not sin again.

Create in me a pure heart, O God, and renew a steadfast spirit within me...Restore to me the joy of your salvation and grant me a willing spirit, to sustain me. (Psalm 51:10,12)

Dear friend, if you are in a place right now where you have given up doing what is right, I encourage you to get back on track. If you ask Him, God will renew the steadfastness of your spirit, breathing life into the glowing embers of your desire to do right. He will give you the strength to stand firm, holding on to what is pure and true.

No Compromise

"What is truth?" These famous words, uttered by Pontius Pilate a little over 2000 years ago, could not be a more fitting question for our times. The postmodern world cries, "truth is what you make it!" The Christian equivalent has become, "the Bible is open to interpretation" (incidentally, every time I have heard a believer use this argument, the part of the Bible they had an issue with was a passage relating to sin!). How refreshing it is then, how countercultural, to believe in absolute truth! How wonderful to have the fixed point, the firm anchor of the unchanging Word. In a world that believes morals evolved for human survival, and that wrong and right has as many interpretations as the earth's billions of inhabitants, there can still be an absolute moral standard.

"But, there are many modern ethical dilemmas not covered in the Bible," some might say. In such instances, we have the Holy Spirit's guidance, working in partnership with the Word. We are assured that He has written wrong and right onto our hearts (see Hebrews 10:16), and will guide us into all truth (see John 16:13). In some cases, when it seems that the Bible is silent on an issue, it can be found under another topic. We can know definitively, for example, that abortion is wrong because it falls under the sixth commandment, "You shall not murder." Even futuristic practices, such as human cloning, are covered in the Bible; *"Your bodies are temples of the Holy Spirit"* (1 Corinthians 6:19).

Moving past humanism and our own arguments, we need to read the Word with eyes of faith, taking at face value the simple truth it contains. When we embrace how black and white the Bible's standards really are, we can start getting free from compromise! We no longer have to justify sinful behavior (which is a tiring business). We can freely confess our sins, falling into the arms of Grace with confidence. As we allow the unadulterated light of the Word to shine on every area of our lives, all darkness will evaporate.

"Dangerous" Surrender

Usually, when we continue to sin and live in compromise, it is because we want to stay the rulers of our own "kingdoms." Not wanting to be "dethroned," we resolve to keep our independence and live our own way. In some ways, modern Christianity has re-enforced this mindset, by emphasizing *mateship* with God over His *Lordship*. Only through surrender, however, can we can see the fullness of God's will unfold in our lives. When we give ourselves wholly to Him, allowing His power to work in us, we will naturally begin to bear spiritual fruit. Conversely, a *lack* of fruit is evidence that we are not completely surrendered to Christ. True acceptance of His Lordship is more than lip-service, it is backed up by action—righteousness and obedience, walking hand in hand:

> Not everyone who says to me, 'Lord, Lord,' will enter the kingdom of heaven, but only the one who does the will of my Father who is in heaven. (Matthew 7:21)

Forgive Without Quarter

When we think of walking in righteousness, perhaps forgiveness doesn't immediately spring to mind. I have included it here, however, because there is no way we can begin to walk in holiness and freedom without it. Forgiveness is like spiritual "Drano," unblocking and clearing away debris from our hearts.

Lying...4. Murder...10. Unforgiveness...3. Violence...7. Years ago, I believed the lie that sins are somehow graded. High up on the list were sins like murder and rape. At the other end of the scale were "smaller" sins, such as bearing a grudge. What I have learned since then, is that sin is *sin*. Unforgiveness is not a "little" sin. Not only does it poison our hearts, but it can endanger our very souls. This revelation shocked me as a student completing my final year of high school. My Biology teacher, who was a strong Christian, showed our class a documentary that would forever change my perspective of unforgiveness—the testimony of Nigerian Pastor Daniel Eekechukwu.[63]

After being involved in a horrific car crash on his way to work, Daniel was fatally injured. He was pronounced dead in an ambulance and taken to the mortuary, where his body was embalmed and prepared for burial. The story would have ended there, were it not for his wife Nneka, a woman of incredible faith. She refused to accept that Daniel was dead and held onto the promise; *"women received back their dead, raised to life again"* (Hebrews 11:35).

So convinced was Nneka that God would raise her husband to life, that she arranged for Daniel's body to be transported to a Reinhard Bonnke crusade. The corpse was carried in a coffin to a church basement below the meeting, where a group of pastors had gathered to pray. As they prayed and massaged Daniel's hands, already stiff with rigor mortis, life began to flow into his body. After a few minutes, Daniel's spirit returned to him. With a deep breath, he sat up and opened his eyes.

As astounding as this miracle is, it is the other half of the story, what happened to Daniel *while* he was dead, that impacted me the most. During the three days that his body lay in the mortuary, Daniel was shown heaven and hell. Heaven was majestic, perfect beyond description, but hell was filled with unspeakable misery and suffering.

To Daniel's utter shock, an angel told him that, were he to die that day, hell would have been his final destination. When Daniel protested, telling the angel how he had lived righteously for the Lord and served him as a pastor, the angel reminded him of the circumstances surrounding his death. The day before he died, Daniel and his wife had a terrible argument. Nneka asked for forgiveness, but Daniel refused to be reconciled to her. He made up his mind to send her away for one year, to teach her a lesson. On the day of the accident, he was still not on speaking terms with her and left home with his heart bubbling with rage. The angel explained that although Daniel had asked God for forgiveness on his way to work, he had not received it because of the grudge he was still nursing.

Daniel's testimony shook me up, to say the least. It marked a turning point in my thinking. I began to see unforgiveness as God does, and to understand one verse I had never wanted to dwell on for too long:

> For if you forgive other people when they sin against you, your heavenly Father will also forgive you. But if you do not forgive others their sins, your Father will not forgive your sins. (Matthew 6:14–15)

Like cancer, unforgiveness can be a "silent killer." It can be in our hearts for years, slowly eating away at us with bitterness. Of all sins, it is the only one we are told can hinder us from receiving *God's* forgiveness. The parable of the unmerciful servant (see Matthew 18:21–35), shows us how God views unforgiveness. When we refuse to forgive others, we are forgetting the massive debt that God has forgiven us of.

The Ultimate Crime and The Greatest Gift

Maybe you are thinking, "but you have no idea the kind of debts people owe me—they are not 'small' ones. The man who raped me owes me my mental health. The boss whose malpractice landed my innocent husband in jail owes us our family back. The woman who stole thousands from us owes us our financial stability. I hold myself to ransom for the mistakes I have made and regrets I have."

If this is you, Dear Friend, my heart aches for the losses you have suffered and the pain you have endured. Without making light of what you have been through, allow me to ask you a simple question—what is the worst crime that one human being can commit against another? To torture them? Or maybe to completely assassinate another's character, tearing their reputation to shreds (bear with me here). Could be to expose them publicly to humiliation, in the cruelest of ways—or perhaps, to take away their very life?

I would submit to you that the crucifixion was the ultimate crime—it was all of these things and much more, in one slow, horrific event. There was no pain so excruciating, no humiliation so public, and no evil as potent as the atrocity committed against Jesus at the cross. There is a reason why Jesus' death was so horrific—it atoned for the full spectrum of every imaginable sin. Because Jesus endured the cross, we have been given the power to forgive. He did not owe anything and yet paid the ultimate price for sins He did not commit. What's more, as Jesus hung dying on the cross, the weight of humanity's penalty pressing upon him, He forgave those who *did* deserve punishment, the very ones who nailed Him there!

Dear Friend, it was *our sin* that put Jesus on the cross, just as much as the people who have wronged us, regardless of the magnitude of their offense. Isaiah 53:6 tells us that *"We all, like sheep, have gone astray, each of us has turned to our own way; and the Lord has laid on him the iniquity of us all."* In effect, to refuse to forgive is like claiming that Christ's sacrifice was enough for us, but not enough for someone else. It is to deny the fullness of the cross. If Jesus could forgive us, as well as the people who hurt us, then we can also forgive: *"Freely you have received, freely give"* (Matthew 10:8).

Don't Let the Sun go Down

Before we leave the topic of forgiveness, let us look at a key step we can take to walk in it on a daily basis—not letting the sun go down while we are still angry (see Ephesians 4:26). This principle is like doing a routine check on the "engine light" of our hearts.

The importance of making forgiveness a practice was impressed on me in an unusual way, several years ago. Alejandro and I were newlyweds living in Warragul, a beautiful country town an hour away from the city of Melbourne, Australia. After eight months of traveling and ministering internationally, we felt led to settle down. This meant swapping a life on the road for the rolling green hills of Victoria's dairy country. I worked as a secondary teacher in nearby town, while Alejandro continued to travel and minister. On this particular occasion, he was away in the United States.

It was a quiet evening and I had just finished a video-chat with Alejandro.

Despite the stillness, however, I felt uneasy, unable to shake off what had just transpired. After an intense "discussion" with Alejandro, I had hung up on him. He tried to call back several times, but I refused to answer. Eventually, he must have given up—the ringtone ceased and the house fell silent once more. Trying to take my mind off the discomfort, I began to tidy up the kitchen and get ready for bed. As I walked from the bedroom to the kitchen, I heard a low rumbling noise—much like the trucks we regularly heard passing by on the highway. As the noise became louder, the ground began trembling so noticeably that I realized it couldn't possibly be a truck. My confused mind scrambled for another explanation—the roof was shaking now, so perhaps it was a jumbo jet flying overhead at low altitude. No wait, that was impossible—we lived over an hour and a half away from the airport!

The ground wrenched out from under my feet, rocking violently from side to side, like a sieve sifting flour. At this point, my mind completely ran out of possibilities. Panicked, I ran from room to room, the words tumbling out of my mouth, "Jesus, help me! Jesus, JESUS!" I am sure, at this point, that *you*, my reader, know exactly what was happening. To someone who grew up in Australia though, (i.e. in a country with very little seismic activity) the last thing I would ever have thought of was an *earthquake*. When it finally dawned on me, I raced to get under a door frame. Halfway there, the shaking suddenly stopped.

I stood frozen on the spot, my heart feeling like it was about to explode—desperately trying to take in what had just happened. I would later discover that I had experienced a 5.4 magnitude quake, the epicenter just 30kms away.

Suddenly a new sensation hit me—the overwhelming desire to get in touch with my husband, to tell him I loved him and to be reconciled with him. I was struck by the sheer enormity of the separation between us, in a way I had not felt before. I became acutely aware, not just of the physical distance between us—but of the emotional and spiritual separation caused by my unforgiveness. The state of my heart was laid painfully bare.

With shaking hands, I tried to call Alejandro. His phone rang for what seemed like an eternity, before forwarding to his voicemail. I tried many more times that night to contact him, but it was too late. He had boarded a plane and would not be contactable until morning. Every small aftershock that night made it feel like the longest of my life! When I was finally able to speak with Alejandro the next morning, I immediately asked for his forgiveness. From this experience came much good—I resolved, with God's help, to never again let resentment or unforgiveness linger in my heart.

Be Loosed!

Jesus warned us that the day of the Lord will come "like a thief in the night" (1 Thessalonians 5:2)—just like the earthquake I experienced. To be fully ready, we need to make forgiveness not only a habit but a lifestyle. Forgiveness must become to us like a broom in the "house" of our hearts, ensuring it is swept out regularly and kept free of bitterness.

I encourage you, beloved, to examine your heart today. Ask the Holy Spirit to reveal to you if there is any area in you have not dealt with and if there is any person you are harboring unforgiveness toward. Remembering that the power of repentance is released through confession, verbalize your forgiveness. As you confess, remember that forgiveness, like love, is a decision—not a feeling. No matter what you feel, determine in your heart to let go of all resentment. A practical way to walk in your newfound freedom is to resolve not to speak of the offense again. It will only renew the pain and hinder the healing process.

I declare that as you confess your forgiveness and release the person who hurt you from all debt, you will begin to experience a freedom beyond anything you have ever known!

❖ ❖ ❖

Chapter 21

Check #4:
Am I Standing on the Word?

Not long ago, I watched an impacting video clip that had been circulating on the internet. Recorded in one of China's underground churches, it shows the moment a box of Bibles is delivered. The instant the box is laid on the ground, dozens of believers run to it, scrambling to claim their copy. Cradling the Bible in their hands, many weep as they tenderly kiss and caress the cover. One man takes the plastic wrap off as carefully as if he were unwrapping a priceless artwork. "This is what we needed," a woman sobs, "this is what we needed *most*."[64] Although I have seen this clip many times, I still can't help but cry. I am struck by the value that these precious brothers and sisters place on the Word. The next thing that strikes me is the contrast between the these believers' desperation for the Word and how the Bible is often treated in the West. Most Western believers have at least one copy of the Bible in their possession, even several. But how many of these Bibles spend most of their days on a shelf, collecting dust?

Once had a vivid dream, that I was living in a two-story house. The odd thing was that the house was built on a slope, right inside the rim of a volcano! The volcano began to erupt, and streams of molten lava crept through the lower floor. I managed to get out just before this happened, but as I stood watching about twenty yards away, a sudden thought occurred to me. I realized that I had left my Bible behind. Without thinking, I ran back into the house. I somehow managed to find my Bible and get out, avoiding the lava. The dream ended there and I found myself wide awake.

When I asked God what the dream meant, He spoke to me about how much we are to treasure the Word and how vital it is, especially when facing the hazards of these days. We must not leave the Word behind when the going gets tough. It is our weapon and our oxygen as we negotiate the world each day:

> For the word of God is alive and active. Sharper than any double-edged sword, it penetrates even to dividing soul and spirit, joints and marrow; it judges the thoughts and attitudes of the heart. (Hebrews 4:12)

The Bible dream happened at a stage in my life when I was just starting to delve into the Word and to understand that I could hear from God. A patchwork of highlighter markings and notes in an old Bible of mine bear testament to this season. Although it is tattered and torn, still covered in the garish wrapping paper I put on it in as a teenager, I cannot bear to part with this precious Bible. When I read through it, I see God's faithfulness documented on each page. Perhaps you also have an old Bible like mine, one whose battered appearance speaks of the spiritual battles you have faced, and whose pages are wrinkled with the tears of sadness and victory.

A Prophetic Map Book

At the beginning of 2015, the Lord spoke to Alejandro and I, clearly telling us that our time in Australia was coming to an end and that we were to begin making arrangements to move to the USA. It would have been a complete shock to me, were it not for God's Word. Amazingly, even before Alejandro and I were married or were in a relationship, the

Lord showed me that I would one day move to the other side of the world.

As I prayed one day, I had asked God for confirmation about whether or not to enter into a relationship with Alejandro (I did not want to proceed without knowing if it was God's will.) Suddenly, I felt led to read a passage about my namesake. As I read where Rebekah was asked if she would marry Isaac, one phrase jumped out at me, *"'Will you go with this man?' 'I will go,' she said,"* (Genesis 24:58). In that instant, the Lord spoke to me, revealing that if I married Alejandro I would one day move to a faraway place. "Will *you* go with this man?" I sensed God ask. I said that I was willing to and felt a deep peace wash over me.

The Word is our prophetic map book, showing us the way we must go—and not just when we are making important life decisions, or facing severe obstacles. We must learn to use the Word in *all* situations (yes, even more than Google!). His Word will continually guide our paths; *"Your word is a lamp for my feet, a light on my path"* (Psalm 119:105).

To ensure that we are grounded in the Word, we must be committed to reading it on a regular basis—not just with our eyes but with our *hearts*. The Word consists of the *logos* and the *rhema* word. Have you ever read the Bible and felt like you were reading a textbook, like the words in front of you were completely lifeless? Without the rhema word, the words stay flat on the page. The rhema is the spoken, God-breathed revelation of His Word. When the Holy Spirit illuminates the Word to our hearts, He causes it to speak directly to us. Have you ever listened to a sermon and felt as though the preacher was speaking only to you? That is the rhema word in action. If you feel stuck in a rut, like God is not speaking to you, I encourage you to ask the Holy Spirit to make His rhema word come alive to you. Continue to ask Him and do not give up. Before long, you will begin to hear God's voice, as He reveals the Word to your spirit.

❖ ❖ ❖

Chapter 22

Check #5: Am I Fulfilling the Great Commission?

When asked what holds them back from boldly proclaiming the gospel, many believers say "fear"—the fear of facing a hostile response, the fear of rejection, the fear of not having all the answers. Whatever the cause, when we allow fear to hinder us from fulfilling the Great Commission, it becomes a stumbling block. To break the stronghold of fear, we must allow God's perfect love to cast it out (see 1 John 4:18). In the context of sharing the gospel, this means we are compelled by God's love to see past people's rejection. One of God's great generals, David Wilkerson, was a living example of this. He stood firm in the face of death threats, reaching out to gang member Nicky Cruz in love. Because Wilkerson's love went deeper than fear, Cruz and many others were won to Christ. Nicky eventually went on to become one of the great evangelists of our time.

"But I'm not called to full-time evangelism," you may think. Perhaps you are not even sure what God's calling for your life is. You can begin to discover that calling, however, right now, at the starting point for all callings—it is *souls*. God always has souls in His sight, no matter the calling. In a way, we are *all* called to full-time evangelism. Whether it be at work, college, at the supermarket or at the playground with our kids, we are all roving evangelists. We have the Greatest Evangelist of all time living inside of us—Jesus Christ. The Word has already outlined for us our life's mission and God's will for us on earth:

> Then Jesus came to them and said, "All authority in heaven and on earth has been given to me. Therefore go and make disciples of all nations, baptizing them in the name of the Father and of the Son and of the Holy Spirit, and teaching them to obey everything I have commanded you. And surely I am with you always, to the very end of the age." (Matthew 28:18–20)

We must understand that the call to evangelism is not just for those who are "in ministry." Ministry comes from the Greek word *diakoneo*—simply meaning, "to serve"[65] or, *douleuo*, meaning "to serve as a slave."[66] In the New Testament, ministry is any service rendered to God or others in Jesus name. When we share the gospel with a person, we are committing an act of service by ministering to them.

I feel it is worth noting here, however, that sharing the gospel is an act that must be accompanied by word. The famous quote by St. Francis of Assisi, "Preach the gospel always, and if necessary, use words," has often been used to espouse evangelizing by lifestyle alone. While the basic principle seems good, for the gospel to be clearly outlined and understood, the Word must also be articulated with words. Please understand that I am *not* speaking as one who never struggles in the area of evangelism. Even as I write, I am personally convicted to make evangelism a way of life. I think of the opportunities I have let slip by in the past and I am challenged to step out in faith.

It may help when witnessing to others to realize that many non-believers are already questioning the world's events. Just a few days ago, my mum had the opportunity to witness to a man who was out walking his dog, simply by asking him, "What do you think of everything happening in the world today?" The man shook his head, saying, "I think it's terrible." Seizing the opportunity, my mum explained how

Revelation speaks of the things we are seeing today and told him how he could receive Christ. While the man did not make a decision for Jesus that day, he listened thoughtfully to all she had to say. My mum walked away from the conversation knowing that she had planted a seed. She prayed that one day he would remember her words and call upon the name of the Lord.

Dear Friends, it is not our responsibility to make someone accept our message—only to deliver it. We did not write the message, we are only the messengers, delivering it on our King's behalf. This is freeing to know because it relieves us of the fear of rejection. When people reject our message, they are not rejecting us, but God; *"Therefore, anyone who rejects this instruction does not reject a human being but God, the very God who gives you his Holy Spirit"* (1 Thessalonians 4:8).

As Jesus hung dying on the cross, He not only bore the weight of our sins, He bore the world's rejection of him. The Word tells us that we have been crucified with Christ and that we no longer live, but Christ in us (see Galatians 2:20). Since we were bought at a price and our lives are no longer ours (see 1 Corinthians 6:20), then we have nothing to be afraid of. Our pride cannot be hurt, nor our self-worth eroded when someone rejects our message. It is impossible to kill a "dead man."

To begin the task of evangelism, we need to be willing to be knocked back, even many times. Success in evangelism is not about numbers, it is about *obedience*. Noah's obedience to evangelize stands as an example to us. We can imagine people approaching Noah, wanting to know what he was building. Noah, as a *"preacher of righteousness"* (2 Peter 2:5), would have given them the opportunity to repent and be saved. For decades, Noah warned people– without seeing a single salvation. He is also described in the Word as a righteous man, blameless among the people of his time, one who walked with God (see Genesis 6:9). Undoubtedly, Noah is honored, not because of the success he had as an evangelist, but for his obedience, even when no one was listening. Jesus warned us that the end times will be *"as the days of Noah"* (Matthew 24:37). This in mind, let us imitate Noah by seizing every opportunity we have to share the gospel, with as many as possible.

No Panic on the Titanic

In 1912, one of the most famous of all maritime disasters took place—the untimely sinking of the RMS Titanic. While it is well known that an iceberg caused the tragedy, not many know that the ship was in trouble long before she sank. Historical accounts reveal that even as the Titanic set sail on her maiden voyage, a fire raged deep inside her hull. One of the coal bunkers had caught fire and a team of firefighters were assigned to keep the blaze under control. The plan was to do so until the Titanic reached New York, where the bunkers could be emptied and the fire could be fully extinguished.

Amazingly, none of the passengers knew of the fire. 1,317 souls slept in their cabins each night, completely unaware of the danger below them. Not wishing to alarm passengers, the ship's officers warned the stokers to keep quiet. The prerogative of maintaining order and avoiding panic prevailed again when the Titanic struck an iceberg. When the first-class passengers were asked to put on life jackets, they were told it was simply "a precaution" and were not informed the ship was actually sinking. The stewards moved about calmly, showing no signs of urgency. As a result, many thought the whole thing to be a joke and refused to come out on deck, preferring the warmth of their cabins to the cold night air. Passengers returned to their cigarettes, card games and conversations, just as the people in my dream ignored Jesus and continued about their business.

Only when the Titanic began to list noticeably to one side, did some finally board the lifeboats. Because of their initial reluctance, however, the first few lifeboats to leave the Titanic were not filled to capacity. Had the officers and stewards not spared passengers the reality of the situation from the beginning, more might have been saved.

Sounding the Alarm

The Titanic disaster bears many parallels to our Christian lives.

The "ship" we are on represents the world and we are the "stewards," those who are aware of the world's ultimate plight. The destruction sin has wreaked upon the earth is like the damage done to the Titanic by the iceberg and fires. Our job is to urge the lost to get into the "lifeboat" of salvation.

This is where we face a dilemma. If we want to maintain order and preserve the status quo, we may be able to lead a few to the "lifeboats," but many will remain unfazed. We are required to love fiercely, even aggressively. It is, sadly, possible to "love" people– right to the gates of hell. To effectively reach people, we need to present the gospel in a way that is not only loving, but causes people to become aware of their need for a Savior. Ironically, although it is love that compels us to confront the sinner with their sin, it is also love that ultimately covers that sin; *"Whoever turns a sinner from the error of their way will save them from death and cover over a multitude of sins"* (James 5:20).

How Deep Is Your Love?

Jesus gives us the ultimate example of going the extra mile to rescue the lost. Was He afraid to go through with His part in the plan of salvation? I believe He was, without a doubt. Jesus, the hundred-percent-divine Jesus, the Son of God said, *"Not my will but yours be done."* Jesus, the hundred-percent-man Jesus, was so distressed that He sweated blood. Yes, sweated *blood.* Not simply a figure of speech, the Bible speaks of a rare but very real condition, called *hematohidrosis.* Interestingly, the physician Luke is the only person to have documented Jesus' bloodied sweat in his gospel.

Modern doctors note that hematohidrosis causes the blood vessels around the sweat glands to rupture, a phenomenon thought to be brought on by extreme stress and anxiety. There have been other historical accounts of individuals sweating blood, for example, Leonardo Da Vinci's description of a soldier sweating blood before going out onto the battlefield. We can gather from this that, a) Jesus was capable of feeling intense fear and, b) that He was so determined to follow through the plan of salvation that His body had literally already started to die, even before He was taken away to be crucified.

I think of the lyrics of that popular 1970's song, "How deep is your love?" We already know the depth of Jesus' love for us—a love that went to the cross, to the very pit of hell to win our souls. We then need to ask ourselves the same question—"how deep is *my* love?" Is it a love only as deep as polite conversation? Or is it a love that pushes past offense and rejection to reach the heart of man? Is it a skin-deep kind of love, one that is easily embarrassed, or is it a love totally emptied of self, willing to be insulted for the gospel? Is our love earth-bound, or heaven-set? Is it the kind of love that is stronger than death? We cannot, of course, summon up this kind of supernatural love in our own humanity. It has to come from God himself.

If you struggle with evangelizing, it's ok. Understand that the struggle itself is not a sin—as long as we are here on earth we wrestle against our own human nature, a nature that is bent on self-preservation. What's *not* okay is to let that nature dominate us, or to get comfortable with it.

To deny your call to evangelism is like having the cure for AIDS hidden in a bottle under your bed. Allow the revelation of Jesus' sacrifice on the cross to drive you to evangelize. As you do so, with every person you reach, the freer you will get. It will become easier each time to witness to others, as you become a sharp tool in God's hands.

Dear Friend, we are almost out of time. The ship is sinking fast and the world groans with the weight of sin. We must go and wake up the souls still asleep in their cabins, urging them to get into the lifeboats. The eternal destiny of millions is hanging in the balance, and we are in a position to do something about it.

How, then, can they call on the one they have not believed in? And how can they believe in the one of whom they have not heard? And how can they hear without someone preaching to them? (Romans 10:14)

❖ ❖ ❖

Chapter 23

Check #6: Am I Prepared for Persecution and Hardship?

Of all the topics I have felt led by the Lord to write about, persecution has been the most difficult. Were I to leave it out, though, this message would be hugely incomplete. As I mentioned earlier, I am unable to slot my theological beliefs into a neat category–pre-tribulation, mid-tribulation, pre-millennial, post-millennial or post-tribulation etc. If the Rapture will be followed by the second coming of Christ, or if the two are one event, I cannot say. That is not to say that I am opposed to developing more definite convictions as God leads but at this point, I feel peace about not knowing the full picture; about accepting the secret things that belong to God (see Deuteronomy 29:29). Just as I will one day look on the face of my Savior and know Him fully, one day I will be able to look back on the narrative of Revelation, with the absolute clarity of retrospect:

> For now we see only a reflection as in a mirror; then we shall see face to face. Now I know in part; then I shall know fully, even as I am fully known. (1 Corinthians 13:12)

When studying Revelation, it is important to avoid, "majoring on the minors." After all, what is more important—to know exactly *how* the End Times will unfold, or to have our hearts *ready* for whatever might ensue? When a soldier goes into battle, he does not prepare for a "soft" fight. A soldier is trained to the highest level, to deal with any scenario he could possibly face. We must be armed with the same attitude. Although none of us can say we know exactly how this last chapter of earth's history will play out, our job is to be ready, to be spiritually armed and prepared.

Despite not subscribing to a particular interpretation, I will say this: I am deeply concerned about the popular belief that, before the "going gets tough," we will be whisked away. "Oh, but we won't be there when that happens," some may say. Even if a pre-tribulation rapture *is* imminent, however, we must still be prepared for trials. The Bible is clear that Christians *will* encounter intense persecution and hardship in the last days:

> Then you will be handed over to be persecuted and put to death, and you will be hated by all nations because of me. At that time many will turn away from the faith and will betray and hate each other, and many false prophets will appear and deceive many people. Because of the increase of wickedness, the love of most will grow cold, but the one who stands firm to the end will be saved. (Matthew 24:9–13)

It is interesting to note in this passage that:

1) Jesus was not just addressing His immediate disciples; He was speaking prophetically to end-time believers.
2) Jesus speaks of some of the types of suffering believers will experience in the last days (martyrdom, persecution, confusion, betrayal, hatred etc.).
3) Jesus urges *believers* to endure to the end and be saved.

This begs the question—if believers are guaranteed a smooth end-time experience, why would we be warned of hardship and admonished to *endure*? No one *endures* watching a pleasant movie, relaxing in a hammock, or eating a delicious meal. Jesus' address to the disciples sounds like that of a president or prime minister sending off his troops to war. Hardship and endurance are also an inseparable theme in Jesus' letters to the churches of Revelation and in Peter's letter to the churches in Asia minor.

"...hold on to what you have until I come. To the one who is victorious and does my will to the end, I will give authority over the nations." (Revelation 2:25–26)

These have come so that the proven genuineness of your faith—of greater worth than gold, which perishes even though refined by fire—may result in praise, glory and honor when Jesus Christ is revealed. (1 Peter 1:7)

It is important to note here that there is a difference between experiencing suffering in the last days and experiencing the wrath of God. When the Israelites lived in Egypt, for example, they experienced a suffering from being under a regime hostile to the Spirit of God (an Old Testament antichrist spirit, if you will). This type of oppression happened when Pharaoh forced the Israelites to make bricks without straw. The plagues, on the other hand, passed over the Israelites, because they were not under God's wrath. We are not appointed to wrath, but we live in a world that is increasingly hostile to the Spirit of God. For this reason, we can expect hardship and persecution.

One Family

Resist him, standing firm in the faith, because you know that the family of believers throughout the world is undergoing the same kind of sufferings. (1 Peter 5:9)

For the pastor whose church has been burnt to the ground, for the parents whose child has been kidnapped by a terrorist organization, or for the believer who risks execution for possessing a Bible, suffering is more than theory—it is a brutal daily reality. These are our brothers and sisters. May we not allow the geographical distance between us to harden our hearts with apathy. For those who are in the thick of it, experiencing great tribulations, end-time persecution is well and truly already here.

A time of testing is coming that we must all be prepared for. In many ways, it has already begun, albeit in its infancy. Over the last decade or so, Christians in the West have already begun to see a notable increase in persecution on home soil. The good news is this—that suffering and persecution have the potential to bring about tremendous spiritual blessings, such as greater maturity, a deeper move of God and growth (spiritually, in our personal lives, and in the church).

Think for a moment what happens to a ball of dough when rolled out with a rolling pin. Rather than being diminished or damaged, the dough spreads out, becoming "enlarged." In the same way, persecution and suffering have the potential to "enlarge," rather than squash us.

A Syrian Pastor writes of this type of spiritual growth, in a letter to International Christian agency, "Open Doors." Sounding much like a soldier's field report, it reads:

I have a huge hope. There is an amazing work happening in my country. The Spirit is moving. We are in a race, a battle. We need to be like the Good Samaritan—get off the donkey, put ourselves in danger and pay in advance...We will be stronger than Satan. We have a long-term strategy. We've seen victories...I want to leave in your hearts this passion: don't at one moment think the church in Syria or Iraq can achieve all this. Nor in Lebanon. Nor in Jordan. We need the whole church. In Revelation it shows Christ's triumph over Satan. That's our prayer."[67]

Dr. Michael Brown echoes these sentiments, projecting them into America's future:

...In that persecution is the hope that awaits America. As the persecution grows, the Church will be forced to return to God's principles of love, obedience, justice, holiness, compassion, truth, and faithfulness. The Church in America will once again become the salt and light that Jesus told us we are supposed to be. And when all is said and done, I believe that revival will come to America. And that revival can spread to the world.[68]

It Comes with the Territory

The idea then that those in the Western church will somehow evade persecution and hardship is incompatible with the Word, to say the least. And yet, such a belief is surely the outworking of the humanistic and modern grace gospels. It is not hard to see how the love of many to grow cold, (see Matthew 24:12) when the going gets tough. If God's love for us *only* means that He wants us to be happy, then the presence of trials in our lives will cause us confusion and doubt. On the other hand, if we see hardship as part of the battle we face as believers, we can look trials in the eye with confidence, rather than running from them.

To accept that hardship is part of the Christian life does not mean to adopt a resigned, defeated attitude. It is not akin to laying in front of a steamroller. On the contrary, the prospect of challenges and enemy attacks should inspire us to rise up in the power of the Spirit. We should not be surprised when, as the Enemy's time grows shorter, his efforts to fight against us grow more intense. Even so, we can face anything and push through any situation, because of the grace God extends to us. For each trial we face, there is an even greater grace available to us—

which explains why Christians who face martyrdom are able to look death in the eye, unafraid. We must arm ourselves with the knowledge that anything that could ever come against us has already been defeated on the cross.

Moving from Patience to Endurance

As the world grows darker around us, we need to make a significant shift in our thinking—from patience to perseverance. Patience waits for a problem to be resolved, while perseverance gives us the strength to keep going indefinitely.

Imagine, for a moment, a man stranded on a desert island (think "Castaway" or "Robinson Crusoe"). When he arrives on the island, he is naïve and unprepared—his only desperate aim to be rescued. There are only two options in his mind: to be rescued, or death. The man spends his first day on the island constructing a huge sign in the sand, hoping to attract the attention of a plane. He waits for hours, before realizing he is extremely thirsty. If he is to survive until a plane comes, he must stay hydrated. He manages to find water, then food, before turning his attention to building a shelter.

As the days progress into weeks, the man's mentality begins to shift. As it becomes apparent that he may be on the island for a long time, his thoughts turn more and more from being rescued to his survival. He becomes savvier and more resilient over time, developing new skills. Two years later, his perseverance pays off. A plane spots him and he is rescued.

In a similar fashion, we can say, "I want out!" when the going gets tough—or we can fasten our spiritual seatbelts and prepare ourselves for a possible long-haul journey. The only difference, of course, between our spiritual survival and the castaway analogy, is that our spiritual survival depends on our trust in God, rather than our own savviness. Even before suffering arises, we must determine in our heart to be like Job, refusing to deny our faith no matter what. Remember, even when the Enemy wanted to come against Job, he had to ask God's permission first (see Job 1:6–12). God does not send evil, nor is He the author of suffering—but until sin is removed from the earth, Satan will continue to launch attacks against God's chosen people.

Eternity in our Hearts

To stay grounded and be able to withstand hardship, we must have our sights set firmly on eternity— *"We have this hope as an anchor for the soul, firm and secure. It enters the inner sanctuary behind the curtain"* (Hebrews 6:19). To stoke the fires of eternity in our hearts, we must be committed to growing in the Word and in our intimacy with God. If we are faithful in doing so, "the things of earth will grow strangely dim," as the old hymn says. Eternity will become more real to us than anything we could touch, see or experience on earth.

Here is one way you can test yourself, to see if you are developing an eternal perspective: ask yourself, in all honesty—if something was to happen to my house today, and everything in it was destroyed (e.g. through a natural disaster), would I have truly "lost everything?" As you imagine the scenario, also ask yourself—would I be able to start over again, having peace in the midst of grief? Would I be able to continue trusting God? Such tough questions can give us insight into our own hearts and the value we place on our material, earthly reality, vs. our eternal, incorruptible reality.

If you are currently wading through deep trials, be encouraged Dear Friend, they will not last forever! Your season of trials is just that—a season.

You can know and trust that whatever you pass through *can* be used for good (see Romans 8:28). Refuse to allow a trial rob you of your hope, energy or joy. Rather, plunder the trial, taking as much out of it as you can for good. If this seems impossible, ask God for the strength and supernatural insight you need.

Hardship will either harden you or soften you. It depends on what you are made of. Wax softens in the heat and becomes pliable, but an egg becomes harder. In the economy of heaven, hardship can make us softer and more pliable in God's hands. Some of the most influential Christian leaders in history have simply been people who have allowed God to mold them through intense trials. The great paradox of hardship is this: that even though it is painful, it provides one of the greatest opportunities we could ever have to receive a greater revelation of God's love, even as we cling to Him and seek His face.

❖ ❖ ❖

Chapter 24

Check #7: Am I growing
Daily in a Relationship with God?

A t the heart of our Christian walk is *relationship*. The mark of
a true disciple is *knowing* Jesus (see Matthew 7:21–23). If we
know God, then we know *Love*. If we know Love, we will have great
peace. When we understand that Love is a person and that when He
dwells in us, fear has no room (see 1 John 4:18).

Think for a moment of the perfect kind of person you would want
looking after you, protecting you, and watching out for you. What would
they be like? What characteristics would they possess? Now let's look at
that famous passage about love, found in 1 Corinthians 13, inserting the
word "God" each time the word "love" appears:

> God is patient, God is kind. [He] does not envy, he does not
> boast, he is not proud. God does not dishonor others, he is
> not self-seeking, he is not easily angered, he keeps no record
> of wrongs. God does not delight in evil but rejoices with
> the truth. He always protects, always trusts, always hopes,
> always perseveres. God never fails us. (1 Corinthians 13:4–
> 8, paraphrased)

Suddenly, this passage comes alive as a beautiful portrait of God's character. In these times, keeping our eyes firmly fixed on God's character anchors us, keeping us from becoming discouraged. If living on planet earth is as foreign an environment for God's people as living underwater, then our closeness to Him is like an oxygen tank, enabling us to breathe. He is the perfect being to depend upon and to take care of us.

Making Jesus the Centre

Our hearts become full of the things we feed them, via our minds. If we feed our hearts fearful thoughts, we will become fearful. If we feed our hearts doubt, we will become *faith-less*. To make Jesus our Rock, we must feed our hearts more of Him. We can do so by spending time in His presence.

In his book, "The Five Love Languages," Dr. Chapman speaks of ways that people prefer to give and receive love.[69] These "love languages" are: words of affirmation, acts of service, receiving gifts, quality time and physical touch. Out of these five, most people usually have one dominant language that makes them feel loved. If your love language is gift giving, for example, you feel loved receiving a gift.

If God has a love language, you can bet it is *quality time*. Like words on a huge aircraft banner tow, the gospel proclaims the message "I love you! I want to be with you!" That Mary was commended for sitting at Jesus' feet and simply *being* with Him shows how much our time with spent with the Lord means to Him. The giving of Jesus' life and the splitting of the Temple veil are the ultimate evidence that God desires to be with us.

As you pursue a life of intimacy with God, regularly encountering His presence, your entire life and being will be transformed. The more you seek God, the more you will grow into the likeness of His Son. Have you ever noticed how some married couples begin to talk, and in some instances, even look like each other? They may use similar facial expressions or speak using similar phrases. Such changes usually don't happen consciously, but by osmosis—simply by being around one another. In the same way, when we spend a lot of time with God, we won't have to struggle and strive to grow into the likeness of Jesus, it will just happen.

God is seeking those who want to become like His Son, those who will seek truth and purity above all else, desiring His presence, no matter what the cost. Being like Jesus means that we will be persecuted as He was, but also that we will have the supernatural strength to overcome, as He did.

Chapter 25

❖ ❖ ❖

Check #8:
Am I walking in the Spirit?

To walk in the Spirit means to allow God to inject His "super" into our "natural," everyday lives. It means being aware that we are a hair's breadth away from the spiritual world and discerning how this impacts our lives. To walk in the Spirit is to be continually aware of His presence; to connect and communicate with Him as we take each step.

To live this way, we need to understand that the Holy Spirit is a person, not a force, or feeling. The Holy Spirit will connect you with the very heart of God, and enable you to know Him on a deeper level. He knows the thoughts of God, and is able to make them known to you.

Learning to Walk in the Spirit

Walking in the Spirit is not as complicated you may have been led to believe. It may feel like a struggled in the beginning, especially if you have never been intentional about doing so before, but over time it will get easier. To a child learning to ride a bike, those first wobbly pushes of the pedals are hard work. As she gains confidence, however, the child begins to glide with ease. In the same way that muscle memory develops over time, so we must practice spiritual disciplines. Where we once may have strained to hear from God, we will learn to easily recognize His voice. Where we may have had trouble perceiving His presence, we will become sensitized, instantly aware the moment His anointing descends in a place.

As is the case with most other spiritual blessings, the primary "ingredient" we need to walk in the Spirit is to have *holy desire*. We must long to know Him more, above all else. If you have never done so before, I challenge you to pray this prayer, right now; "Dearest Holy Spirit, I want to know you deeply. Please reveal more of Your supernatural presence to me each day. Help me to hear your voice clearly. Make known to me the heart and thoughts of God, through Christ Jesus."

That's all. Even if you do not immediately sense anything different, determine to continue seeking the Holy Spirit until you lay hold of God's promise. If you feel led to fast, fast. Whatever you do, don't give up. Be patient as you wait, as even Jesus' disciples were directed to be; *"I am going to send you what my Father has promised; but stay in the city until you have been clothed with power from on high"* (Luke 24:49).

The disciples did not receive an outpouring of the Holy Spirit as soon as they met in the upper room. They had to press in and wait on God.

You don't have to ascend a mountain like Moses, however, to experience God's presence. "Pressing in" could mean simply "retreating" to your room on a regular basis, specifically to be alone with the Lord. As you persist, you can be assured of this—He promises to give us more of presence and He delights to give His children good gifts (see Matthew 7:11). His Holy Spirit is goodness personified; there is no better gift we could ask for.

The second "ingredient" we need to walk in the Spirit is *surrender*— the surrendering of our ideas, our way of doing things, and of ourselves. A word of warning here: as you begin to move in the Spirit, expect some form of backlash from your flesh! If your flesh and mind have been used to being in the driver's seat, they will not appreciate suddenly being forced to take a back seat! As their influence wanes, however, a beautiful exchange will take place– of God's infinite knowledge for your limited knowledge, and the Holy Spirit's insight in the place of your natural understanding. The weight of your life, decisions, worries, and stresses will come to rest on God, resulting in glorious freedom and peace.

An Invasion of the Supernatural

As well as inviting the Holy Spirit into your "world," be prepared to accept the invitation to enter His—be willing to allow His supernatural to "invade" your natural, at any given moment. You will see new opportunities open up for God's supernatural power to move in "ordinary" situations. You only need step out in faith, drawing from His power. Is He asking you to pray for the young woman you met at the shops? Then pray for her. Is the Spirit speaking to you about starting a ministry? Then be obedient. Start to move in the right direction.

The Battle is Afoot!

Our call to walk in the Spirit is inextricably linked with our call to spiritual warfare. It pains me to see so many of God's children go through life in a kind of spiritual "fetal position"—curled up in a ball, bearing the brunt of every enemy attack that comes their way. It affects me because I was once in the same position. Paralyzed by fear, I came to believe that my lot in life was to endure the daily torment of panic attacks. Unable to even leave my house some days, I resigned myself to a life controlled by symptoms I could not explain. God had other ideas, however—He broke through my night with the power of His Holy Spirit, and, with the guidance of loving mentors, showed me how to fight. He broke the stronghold of fear off my life and taught me (just as importantly), how to stay free. I learned to walk in authority and in my God-given identity.

To be fully prepared for the times ahead, we must understand that our position as a Christian is not to be on the defensive—that we have real authority to overcome the schemes of the Enemy; *"I have given you authority to trample on snakes and scorpions and to overcome all the power of the enemy; nothing will harm you"* (Luke 10:19).

There is a battle taking place right now in the heavenlies and on earth, one that is intensifying day by day. The Enemy is doing all he can to prolong the inevitable. If we are not walking in the Spirit, we will not be aware of or have the firepower to fight against his strategies. To be effective, we need to fight spirit with *the* Spirit:

> For our struggle is not against flesh and blood, but against the rulers, against the authorities, against the powers of this dark world and against the spiritual forces of evil in the heavenly realms. (Ephesians 6:12)

Warfare 101

While we do not have the time here to cover spiritual warfare in great depth, let us look at the fundamentals, in a nutshell. Firstly, human strategies, without the power of the Spirit, are useless. We can rebuke until we are hoarse, but if we are not, a) being led by the revelation of the Spirit and, b) clothed with the His anointing, then no demon in hell will budge. The seven sons of Sceva discovered this the hard way:

> One day the evil spirit answered them, "Jesus I know, and Paul I know about, but who are you?" Then the man who had the evil spirit jumped on them and overpowered them all. He gave them such a beating that they ran out of the house naked and bleeding. (Acts 19:15–16)

The demons recognized who carried the anointing and who did not. The Sceva brothers' "exorcism formula" failed miserably because they lacked a true relationship with Jesus and lacked the power of the Holy Spirit. Because of this, they had no real authority to cast out evil. Their literal nakedness symbolized their spiritual vulnerability.

Secondly, it is important when undertaking spiritual warfare to not be limited by what we can see. We must remember that we live across two planes—the spiritual and the natural. Warfare must be guided by the Spirit to be effective. Only the Holy Spirit can give us insight into the true spiritual dynamics of a situation—a "behind the scenes" look, if you will, of what is really going on. Prophetic insight is one of the most powerful weapons we have in warfare. Although a prophet tends to operate in this gifting continually (by virtue of his or her office), prophetic insight is also available to all believers.

Lastly, when we face evil, we must know who we are. Nowhere is it more important to know our identity than when facing a demon or a demonic attack. I recall an occasion, several years ago, when I ministered to a young Korean woman. She was being mentally tormented by the Enemy and we prayed for her freedom. At one point she manifested. Pointing a quivering finger at me, she screamed, "You're pretending!"

One of the benefits of such a blatant spiritual attack is that we become aware of the Enemy's strategies. Like a flash of rifle fire, giving away a sniper's position, her words alerted me to the Enemy's plans to destroy a believer's identity. Satan will often try and erode our authority in Christ by making us doubt who we are in Him.

Have you ever felt like a fraud, perhaps not "spiritual enough" to walk in the fullness of your God-given identity? If so, you may have fallen victim to spiritual "identity theft." You are not alone though, even the Son of God faced the same type of attack. As Jesus stumbled through the desert, starving, the enemy hissed at Him, *"If you are the Son of God..."* (Matthew 4:6). Later in Jesus' life, as He hung dying on the cross, the Enemy tried once again to intimidate Him, saying; *"...save yourself! Come down from the cross, if you are the Son of God!"* (Matthew 27:40) Interestingly, these attempts to undermine Jesus' authority took place at the two most crucial moments in his life. Because Satan was not able to get Jesus to doubt his identity, he could not stop Him from fulfilling His life's mission.

You can walk in confidence, knowing Jesus won back our identity for us on the cross. Because Jesus held out against the enemy and did not waver, His perfect character (not ours), has given us the authority to stand against the Enemy's schemes!

Greater Things

One of the defining characteristics of the last days will be the outpouring of God's Spirit:

> I will pour out my Spirit on all people. Your sons and daughters will prophesy, your old men will dream dreams, your young men will see visions. Even on my servants, both men and women, I will pour out my Spirit in those days. (Joel 2:28–29)

This is wonderful news! Even as the world grows darker around us, we will see the most glorious manifestations of the Spirit's power in history. More than ever, it is time for Jesus' followers to rise up and embrace the *"greater works"* He spoke of in John 14:12; *"Very truly I tell you, whoever believes in me will do the works I have been doing, and they will do even greater things than these, because I am going to the Father."* These prophetic words are truly coming to pass in our lifetimes, as we witness types of miracles never before seen—even during Jesus' earthly ministry.

Take, for example, the story of a young Thai woman named Um, who was involved in a motorcycle collision. Although she survived, Um lost her unborn baby. Just before she was due to have a surgery to remove the child's body, Um decided to attend a weekly prayer service in her village. After receiving prayer, she felt the baby kick inside her. Um went on to deliver a perfectly healthy baby at full term![70]

Jesus raised people from the dead, but who has ever heard of an unborn baby being raised from the dead *in the womb!* I believe we are going to see more of these kinds of miracles—the ones that are completely "out of the box." I believe the times are coming, for example, when we will see some of the same kinds of miracles the Israelites experienced in the desert—the supernatural provision of food and signs in the natural elements. God's power will be made manifest like never before, and the "impossibilities" we face will become a platform for the Spirit to move.

Chapter 26

Having Done Everything, Stand

So now, by God's grace, you are seeking His face with all your heart and learning to walk in the power of His Spirit and in forgiveness. You are praying for discernment and have determined to face whatever trials may come your way with absolute trust in Him. So what now?

The Word tells us that after we have done everything we can, to simply stand:

> Therefore put on the full armor of God, so that when the day of evil comes, you may be able to stand your ground, and after you have done everything, to stand. (Ephesians 6:13)

To stand is not a passive action, but a display of security. It is evidence of our trust in God. It is an internal stance we take, even as we fulfill the will of God in our lives. It is the understanding that every battle we could ever face has already been won. What a beautiful thing that is, to know that no matter how deep the world around us sinks, we have the victory—good has already triumphed over evil and will silence it, once and for all, very soon. Our hearts can be filled with great joy and expectation. Soon we will stand before our precious Father and our Redeemer Jesus Christ! I can't wait!

I remember as a child trying to fall asleep the night before my birthday. The excitement and suspense were unbearable...especially when I had a fair idea of what I would be getting (don't ask me how!) As I lay there, I would think about what it was going to be like to actually own the long-desired gift and hold it in my hands. For hours sleep would evade me before I finally drifted off.

This illustration pales into insignificance, compared to the excitement we should feel at the prospect of all that awaits us, after the final curtain has fallen on this world. I encourage you to often remind yourself that there is an eternal destiny waiting for you that more real, more vivid than anything you have ever known. If you allow this revelation to become your spiritual anchor, it will help keep your whole life in perspective:

> For our light and momentary troubles are achieving for us an eternal glory that far outweighs them all. So we fix our eyes not on what is seen, but on what is unseen, since what is seen is temporary, but what is unseen is eternal. (2 Corinthians 4:17–18)

What a wonderful privilege it is, to have the gift of hindsight– even before the end of all things. We already know the ending. Our struggles will not last forever. To he who waits and hopes, earth is only the prolog to eternity. Let us be filled with hope, remembering Jesus' words; *"When these things begin to take place [in the last days], stand up and lift up your heads, because your redemption is drawing near"* (Luke 21:28).

Revelation Prayer

Today I invite you to pray this prayer, asking God to guide you in the coming days:

> *My precious friend and Father, I love You. I desire to be close to You, more than anything. I take hold of Your*

hand in these times, and I'm not letting go. These days are uncertain, but You are my strength and refuge. Please give me the endurance, peace, and assurance I need, at all times. Sustain me by Your grace and by your Word each day, helping me grow in obedience to You. Thank you, because You promise that You are faithful to complete the work You began in me (Philippians 1:6) and to keep me until the end (1 Thessalonians 5:23–24).

I will not be afraid of whatever lies ahead; I will stand firm, knowing that You have already overcome the world (John 16:33). Rid my heart of all unforgiveness and bitterness, continually cleansing me from unrighteousness. Prepare me for the day when we will finally meet face to face. I ask You to use me as an instrument to reach a dying and hurting world, while there is still time. I surrender myself utterly to You and to Your will in my life. I am Yours. Amen.

Now let us stand firm, holding onto His promises:

And if I go and prepare a place for you, I will come back and take you to be with me that you also may be where I am. You know the way to the place where I am going. (John 14:3–4)

Surely I am with you always, to the very end of the age. (Matthew 28:20)

Appendix I—A Letter to Pastors

Dear Pastor,

We have noticed as we travel that many people in the church have a fascination with the end times. Many are eager to ask questions and know how world events are lining up with Scripture. This is not limited by age; teenagers and even young children are hungry to know "what is going on?" Unbelievers also sense that something "is up" and are searching for the keys to understand what they see. As a pastor, you have the unique task of relaying God's end-time message in an accessible way.

Preaching on Revelation need not be an overly complex or scary experience—(for you, or your congregation!) If you do not feel confident to address all the nuances of Revelation, don't worry—it's ok to just "major on the majors." If your church knows that you are walking a journey of discovery with them, they will generally be gracious. Even if your church dynamics are challenging, I encourage you to move ahead, prayerfully gauging where your people are at, as you build a culture of openness to engage with the end times. One of the steps you can take towards this end is to encourage your congregation to not simply, "take your word for it," but to undertake their own prayerful study of Revelation.

To the pastor holding back from teaching about Revelation because they are concerned about "getting it wrong—" let me say that I completely understand. The burden of writing this book has been immense, particularly with the warning *"if anyone adds [or] takes away from the words of the book of this prophecy..."* (Revelation 22:18–19) always at the forefront of my mind. God is gracious, however, and He understands our motives. If our hearts are in the right place, He will gently correct any misconceptions we may have, even as we ask for greater insight.

Lastly, I encourage you to equip your congregation with practical and spiritual ways they can prepare for the last days, as opposed to a rigid theological framework. A congregation that has the head knowledge of Revelation, but does not understand their personal need for preparation, will ultimately be ill-prepared for the days to come.

May you be filled with joy as you undertake this beautiful task—of preparing the glorious Bride of Christ for His return. When you see Him face to face, may He say to you with a smile, "Well done good and faithful servant."

Yours in Christ,
Rebekah Arias

Appendix II — Endnotes

Chapter 3.

1 Strong's Hebrew Concordance, entry 8251.

2 For more information about The Temple Institute, you can visit https://www. templeinstitute.org

3 The Hebrew University of Jerusalem. "Archaeological Remains Point To Exact Location Of Second Temple Of Jerusalem." ScienceDaily. Accessed December 19, 2016. www.sciencedaily.com/releases/2007/02/070212113227.htm

Chapter 4.

4 Strong's Greek Concordance, entry 3466.

5 United Nations. "About the World Council." Accessed July 30, 2015. http:// www.millenniumpeacesummit.org

6 Bin Muhammad bin Talal, Prince Ghazi. "The ACW Letter." October 13, 2007. Accessed July 30, 2015. http://www.acommonword.com/the-acw-document/

7 European Council of Religious Leaders. "Interreligious Dialogue (Berlin Declaration)." February 16, 2008. Accessed October 18, 2016. http://rfp-europe.eu/interreligious-dialogue-berlin-declaration/

Chapter 5.

8 Biblepaedia. "Nimrod Part 5: From the Works of Flavius Josephus." February 19, 2012. Accessed August 5, 2015. https://biblepaedia.wordpress. com/2012/02/19/nimrod-part-5-from-the-works-of-flavius-josephus/

9 For further information, please see http://en.unpacampaign.org/248/chief-justices-of-global-south-call-for-world-parliament/

10 To view the highlights of an address made by Ban Ki Moon's during the United Nations 70th anniversary commemorative events, please visit http:// www.un.org/apps/news/story.asp?NewsID=52090#.WFlcfxsrKDI

11 3000ad. "European Parliament Building in Strasberg, France." Digital image. Bigstock Photo. Accessed June 6, 2017. https://www.shutterstock.com/image-photo/european-parliament-building-strasbourg-france-24309172

12 Jorisvo. "The Tower of Babel Painting by Pieter Breughel." Digital image. Bigstock Photo. Accessed December 10, 2016. http://www.bigstockphoto.com/ image-32236112/stock-photo-tower-of-babel-%28babylon%29

13 Nguyen, Marie-Lan. "Rape of Europa." Digital image. Wikimedia Commons. Accessed December 10, 2016. https://commons.wikimedia.org/wiki/ File:Rape_of_Europa_MAN_Napoli_Inv111475.jpg

14 MattiaATH. "National Side of Two Euro Coin Issued by Greece." Digital image. Bigstock Photo. Accessed December 10, 2016. http://www. bigstockphoto.com/image-110834474/stock-photo-national-side-of-greece-two-euro-coin-on-black-background

[15] Palm, Jukka. "Bull Depicted as Bas-relief on the Original Ishtar Gate, Ancient Babylon, Iraq." Digital image. Bigstock Photo. Accessed December 10, 2016. http://www.bigstockphoto.com/image-149022908/stock-photo-bull-depicted-as-bas-relief-on-the-original-ishtar-gate%2C-ancient-babylon%2C-iraq

[16] Hofmeester. "Ancient Greek Frieze with Statues of Greek Mythical Beings." Digital image. Bigstock Photo. Accessed December 10, 2016. http://www.bigstockphoto.com/image-9369875/stock-photo-frieze-of-the-pergamon-altar

Chapter 6.
[17] Staff, Telegraph. "Russian Meteor Exploded with Force of 30 Hiroshima Bombs." *The Telegraph*(Telegraph.co.uk), February 16, 2013. http://www.telegraph.co.uk/news/science/space/9874662/Russian-meteor-exploded-with-force-of-30-Hiroshima-bombs.html

[18] Biltz, Mark. *Blood Moons: Decoding the Imminent Heavenly Signs*. Cleveland, OH, United States: WND Books, 2014.

[19] Hagee, John. *Four Blood Moons: Something Is about to Change*. Brentwood, TN: Worthy Publishing, 2013.

[20] Fletcher, Steve. "A Trumpet for My People." April 4, 2014. Accessed August 14, 2014. http://2fletchdr222.blogspot.com.au/2014/04/the-history-of-8-blood-moon-tetrads.html

[21] Williamson, Stephen. "Jubilee Years." Accessed September 11, 2016. http://www.swcs.com.au/jubilees.htm.

Chapter 7.
[22] D. Guha-Sapir, R. Below, Ph. Hoyois - EM-DAT: The CRED/OFDA International Disaster Database :www.emdat.be – Université Catholique de Louvain – Brussels – Belgium.

[23] Ferguson, Niall. *The Cash Nexus: Economics and Politics from the Age of Warfare Through the Age of Welfare, 1700-2000*. New York: Basic Books, 2002. Retrieved from: https://www.amazon.com/Cash-Nexus-Money-Modern-1700-2000/dp/0465023266

[24] Emer, Gibbs. "Emerging Zoonotic Epidemics in the Interconnected Global Community." *The Veterinary Record* 157, no. 22 (November 26, 2005): 673–79. Accessed September 18, 2016. http://www.onehealthinitiative.com/publications/Gibbs_Emer_Zoonotic_%20Wooldridge.pdf

[25] University of Rochester Medical Center. "Support Cells Found in Human Brain Make Mice Smarter - Newsroom - University of Rochester Medical Center." March 7, 2013. Accessed September 18, 2016. https://www.urmc.rochester.edu/news/story/3770/support-cells-found-in-human-brain-make-mice-smarter.aspx

[26] Martin, Daniel and Simon Caldwell. "150 Human Animal Hybrids Grown in UK Labs: Embryos Have Been Produced Secretively for the Past Three Years." *Daily Mail* (DMG Media), November 5, 2011. http://www.dailymail.co.uk/sciencetech/article-2017818/Embryos-involving-genes-animals-mixed-humans-produced-secretively-past-years.html

[27] Kolata, Gina. "National Institutes of Health May Fund Human-Animal Stem Cell Research." *The New York Times* (Arthur Ochs Sulzberger, Jr.), August 4, 2016. http://www.nytimes.com/2016/08/05/health/stem-cell-research-ban.html?_r=1

[28] Ryan, Patrick C. "Zoonoses Likely to Be Used in Bioterrorism." *Public Health Reports* 123, no. 3 (2008): 276. Accessed September 18, 2016. http://www.ncbi.nlm.nih.gov/pmc/articles/PMC2289981/

[29] *Encyclopædia Britannica*. Encyclopædia Britannica, 2016. s.v "Neutron bomb." Accessed September 18, 2016. https://www.britannica.com/technology/neutron-bomb

Chapter 8.

[30] The Associated Press. "FDA Approves Computer Chip for Humans." October 13, 2004. Accessed September 19, 2016. http://www.nbcnews.com/id/6237364/ns/health-health_care/t/fda-approves-computer-chip-humans/#.V99htSgrLNM

[31] Graham-rowe, Duncan. "Clubbers Choose Chip Implants to Jump Queues." May 21, 2004. Accessed April 4, 2015. http://www.newscientist.com/article/dn5022-clubbers-choose-chip-implants-to-jump-queues.html#.VR_85vmUeSo

[32] Gilmore, Heath. "Microchip Implant Ahead of IPhone 6 Release." *Sydney Morning Herald* (Fairfax Media), September 7, 2014. http://www.smh.com.au/technology/sci-tech/microchip-implant-ahead-of-iphone-6-release-20140906-10cx9c.html

[33] This technology is now available. Near Field Communication (NFC) enables smart phones can read microchips at short range, much like contactless payment. This development has the potential to eventually digitize our entire wallets.

[34] Biohacking is the experimental practice of manipulating and modifying biology, for example, by altering the human body using technology.

[35] Cellan-Jones, Rory. "Office Puts Chips Under Staff's Skin." January 29, 2015. Accessed August 29, 2015. http://www.bbc.com/news/technology-31042477

[36] Swain, Frank. "Why I Want a Microchip Implant." February 10, 2014. Accessed August 29, 2015. http://www.bbc.com/future/story/20140209-why-i-want-a-microchip-implant

[37] Verichip. "Verichip Commercial- Health Link". Filmed [May 23, 2008]. YouTube video, 01:03. Posted [Oct 14, 2009]. https://www.youtube.com/watch?v=UDhDrFrs7as

[38] Weissert, Will. "Microchips Implanted in Mexican Officials." July 15, 2004. Accessed September 19, 2016. http://www.nbcnews.com/id/5439055/ns/ technology_and_science-tech_and_gadgets/t/microchips-implanted-mexican-officials/#.V99nWigrLNM

[39] Strong's Greek Lexicon, entry 5480.

[40] Jones, K. C. "Invisible RFID Ink Safe for Cattle and People, Company Says." January 10, 2007. Accessed August 30, 2015. http://www.informationweek. com/invisible-rfid-ink-safe-for-cattle-and-people-company-says/d/d-id/1050602

[41] Christensen, Bill. "Invisible 'radio' Tattoos Could Identify Soldiers." January 19, 2007. Accessed August 30, 2015. http://www.livescience.com/1242-invisible-radio-tattoos-identify-soldiers.html

[42] Gilmore, Heath. "Microchip Implant Ahead of IPhone 6 Release." *Sydney Morning Herald* (Fairfax Media), September 7, 2014. http://www.smh.com.au/technology/sci-tech/microchip-implant-ahead-of-iphone-6-release-20140906-10cx9c.html

Chapter 9.

[43] Cahn, Jonathan. *The Mystery of the Shemitah: The 3, 000-Year-Old Mystery That Holds the Secret of America's Future, the World's Future, and Your Future!* New York, NY, United States: Frontline, 2014.

[44] BBC. "Bear Markets: Wall Street's Worst." *BBC Business* (BBC News), November 1, 2004. http://news.bbc.co.uk/2/hi/business/3746044.stm

[45] Cahn, Jonathan. "The Shemitah's Eerie Mystery of the Sevens." October 31, 2014. Accessed September 4, 2015. http://www.charismanews.com/us/45974-the-shemitah-s-eerie-mystery-of-the-sevens

Chapter 10.

[46] Newport, Frank. "Five Things We've Learned about Americans and Moral Values." June 8, 2015. Accessed September 14, 2015. http://www.gallup.com/opinion/polling-matters/183518/five-things-learned-americans-moral-values.aspx

[47] Newport, Frank. "Americans Continue to Shift Left on Key Moral Issues." May 26, 2015. Accessed September 14, 2015. http://www.gallup.com/poll/183413/americans-continue-shift-left-key-moral-issues.aspx?utm_source=liberal&utm_medium=search&utm_campaign =tiles

[48] MacAskill, Ewen. "Fivefold Increase in Terrorism Fatalities Since 9/11, Says Report." *The Guardian*(The Guardian News and Media), November 17, 2014. http://www.theguardian.com/uk-news/2014/nov/18/fivefold-increase-terrorism-fatalities-global-index

49 United Nations Office on Drugs and Crime. "Trafficking in Children on the Increase, According to Latest UNODC Report." November 24, 2014. Accessed September 14, 2015. https://www.unodc.org/unodc/en/frontpage/2014/November/trafficking-in-children-on-the-increase--according-to-latest-unodc-report.html

50 United Nations Economic and Social Council. "World Crime Trends and Emerging Issues and Responses in the Field of Crime Prevention and Criminal Justice." February 12, 2014. Accessed September 14, 2015. https://www.unodc.org/documents/data-and-analysis/statistics/ crime/ECN. 1520145_EN.pdf

51 Starnes, Todd. "Exclusive: Franklin Graham Warns Gay Marriage Ruling Will Lead to Christian Persecution." *Fox News* (Fox Broadcasting Company), n.d. http://radio.foxnews.com/toddstarnes/top-stories/exclusive-franklin-graham-warns-gay-marriage-ruling-will-lead-to-christian-persecution.html

52 The Christian Broadcasting Network. "Christian Bakers: Ruling Should Scare Every American." July 7, 2015. Accessed September 15, 2015. http://www.cbn.com/cbnnews/us/2015/July/Christian-Bakers-Fined-Gagged-in-Gay-Cake-Case/

53 O'Neil, Tyler. "US Christians at Values Voter Summit: Religious Discrimination in America Is Real, Increasing." October 14, 2013. Accessed September 15, 2015. http://www.christianpost.com/news/us-christians-at-values-voter-summit-religious-discrimination-in-america-is-real-increasing-106591/

54 Fieldstadt, Elisha. "Kim Davis Mocked by 'marriage' Billboard in Her Hometown." *NBC News* (NBC), September 13, 2015. http://www.nbcnews.com/news/us-news/kim-davis-chastised-billboard-erected-her-hometown-n426586

55 Lukianoff, Greg. "FAU College Student Who Didn't Want to Stomp on 'Jesus' Runs Afoul of Speech Code." *Forbes* (Forbes Inc.), March 26, 2013. http://www.forbes.com/sites/realspin/2013/03/26/fau-college-student-who-didnt-want-to-stomp-on-jesus-runs-afoul-of-speech-code/#4e21cbf996fa

56 Barrett, David. "Christians Have No Right to Wear Cross at Work, Says Government." *The Telegraph* (Telegraph Media Group), March 10, 2012. http://www.telegraph.co.uk/news/religion/9136191/Christians-have-no-right-to-wear-cross-at-work-says-Government.html

Chapter 11.

57 Lewis, John. "Thumbs and Toes." Conference Session, Gathering of the Generals, Life Church, Adelaide SA, July, 2015

Chapter 12.

58 The American Humanist Society. "Humanist Manifesto I." 1933. Accessed May 2, 2015. http://americanhumanist.org/humanism/humanist_manifesto_i

Chapter 13.

59 Brown, Michael L. *Hyper-Grace: Exposing the Dangers of the Modern Grace Message*. United States: Charisma House, 2014.

60 Ibid.

61 The Strong's Greek Concordance translates *katharizei* as the continual verb "cleanses," e.g. "His Son cleanses us from all sin" 1 John 1:7, NASB.

62 Strong's Greek Concordance, entry 2716.

Chapter 20.

63 To watch Pastor Daniel Ekechukwu's testimony, you can order a free copy of "Raised from the Dead," from http://www.freecfandvd.org

Chapter 21.

64 International Christian Concern. "Missionary Footage Captures Emotion of Chinese Christians Receiving Bibles for the First Time." *YouTube*. March 17, 2014. Posted September 21, 2016. https://www.youtube.com/watch?v=CkXDcdMNE-I

Chapter 22.

65 Strong's Greek Lexicon, entry 1247.

66 Strong's Greek Lexicon, entry 1398.

Chapter 23.

67 Open Doors. "Syria: 'There is an amazing work happening in my country' - Letter from Pastor." March 14, 2016. Accessed July 10, 2016. http://www.opendoorsuk.org/news/stories/syria_160314.php

68 Jesse, David S. "Dr. Michael Brown Responding to the Coming Persecution." Accessed July 10, 2016. http://davidsjesse.com/dr-michael-brown-responding-to-the-coming-persecution

Chapter 24.

69 Chapman, Gary. *The Five Love Languages: How to Express Heartfelt Commitment to Your Mate*. New York, NY, United States: Thorndike Press, 2005.

Chapter 25.

70 Burnett, Brain and Margaret Burnett. "Transformation in Phuket, Thailand." 2010. Accessed July 10, 2016. http://www.transformourworld.org/en/blogs/399-transformation-in-phuket-thailand

For more information, contact:
AAIM Ministries USA
P.O. Box 120660
Clermont, FL 34712-0060
Phone: (214) 296-4019
Website: www.alejandroarias.net

AAIM Ministries Australia
64 Regal Road
Point Cook, Vic, 3030
Phone: (61) 490-133-453
Website: www.alejandroarias.net